Using Data as a Quality Tool

in Developmental Disabilities

Harness the Power of Your Data

How to Use Data to Promote Quality Improvement in
Developmental Disabilities Service Organizations

Steven D. Staugaitis, Ph.D.
Emily Lauer, MPH
University of Massachusetts Medical School
Center for Developmental Disabilities Evaluation and Research

DEDICATION

This book and the entire *Risk Management in DD* series is dedicated to all the people who happen to have an intellectual disability and who are striving to experience acceptance, dignity and respect in their daily lives.

CONTENTS

ACKNOWLEDGMENTS

This book is part of a series entitled **Risk Management in DD** and is designed to accompany the *Data Analysis for Quality Improvement* course that is available in the online internet-based suite of educational courses available at the University of Massachusetts Medical School's udiscovering.org website. The online courses, in addition to the content contained in the series books, present a number of additional resources including video-based and interactive learning tools that can enhance the educational experience. Both the books and online courses in this series have been specifically designed for personnel who work with and support individuals with intellectual and developmental disabilities within the public and the private service sector, as well as those who have responsibility for monitoring and evaluating these services and supports.

Much of the material contained in this book as well as the entire **Risk Management in DD** series is the result of careful review of national and international practice standards and is based on extensive hands-on experience working within the field of developmental disabilities service by the authors. The content that is included in this book and the approach to risk management that is presented throughout the series is therefore both evidence based and practical. Perhaps of equal importance it is designed for direct application and use by I/DD service providers and systems. Taken together the series represents a "toolbox" for the mitigation of risk and enhancement of quality in services and supports to people with a disability.

The **Risk Management in DD** series of on–line courses was developed with the support of a federal grant from the National Institutes of Health.

NIH Grant Number 5 R42 HD063179-03

FOR MORE INFORMATION
about the **Risk Management in DD** series please visit our website at

http://www.udiscovering.org/

TO LEARN MORE ABOUT THE ON-LINE COURSES
in the **Risk Management in DD** series go to Chapter 1 in this book
or
TO ACCESS THE ON-LINE COURSES GO TO
http://www.udiscovering.org/products/risk-management-developmental-disabilities

Thank you
Steve Staugaitis and Emily Lauer

ABOUT THE AUTHORS

Steven D. Staugaitis, Ph.D.

Dr. Steven Staugaitis is on the faculty of the University of Massachusetts Medical School, Department of Family Medicine and Community Health where he provides support to the E.K. Shriver Center, Center for Developmental Disabilities Evaluation and Research. Steve has over 40 years of direct experience working with individuals with intellectual and developmental disabilities and in administering local, regional and statewide programs and services. He is a licensed clinical psychologist who has managed large I/DD facilities and regional support systems serving people with disabilities. Steve has been a consultant to a variety of state and private provider I/DD organizations within the United States, providing technical assistance, training and support in the areas of risk management, program and systems evaluation and quality assurance and improvement. He has been a principal investigator on a number of federal grants, including a grant from the National Institutes of Health (#5 R42 HD063179-03) that supported the development of the series of on-line courses entitled: *Risk Management in DD*.

Emily Lauer, MPH

Emily Lauer is on the faculty of the University of Massachusetts Medical School, Department of Family Medicine and Community Health and at the E.K. Shriver Center, Center for Developmental Disabilities Evaluation and Research. She has a master's degree in public health in biostatistics. Emily has worked in the field of intellectual and developmental disabilities for over 12 years. She works closely with public and private disability service agencies and government organizations to help them utilize best practice approaches to health and risk surveillance as a tool for implementing targeted improvements to health and service quality. Emily has been collecting and analyzing information on morbidity and mortality trends in people with disabilities for over a decade. Together with Dr. Steven Staugaitis, she has co-authored *Using Data as a Quality Tool in DD* as well as other offerings in the *Risk Management in DD* series of on-line courses and books.

CHAPTER 1

An Introduction to Risk Management
in Developmental Disabilities

Special Note: Chapters 1 and 2 are presented in each of the books and on-line courses in the *Risk Management in DD* series. The first chapter summarizes the course content across the entire series. The material contained in the second chapter (Culture of Safety) represents an important foundation for understanding the complex issues that so often contribute to the adverse events that can result in serious harm and even avoidable death for people with a disability. Understanding these issues is absolutely essential for the enhancement of safety in I/DD services. It is a necessary condition for properly managing risk and improving quality in the I/DD service system. If you have already read this material in one of the other books or courses please skip forward to Chapter 3; or better yet, simply re-review the material in Chapter 2 that you are most interested in.

BAD THINGS HAPPEN. Unfortunately, they seem to happen way too often to people with intellectual and other developmental disabilities. They happen in poor programs and services, they happen in mediocre programs and even in the best programs. Bad things happen when people choose and control their own supports and the people who assist them. Bad things happen even when staff are well screened, trained and supervised. They happen despite managers and advocates reminding everyone to be "vigilant" and to "pay attention." Bad things happen. They happen even though the vast majority of staff are caring and well intentioned people - trying their best to do a very challenging job.

Why is it that "bad things" continue to happen in programs and services that support people with intellectual and developmental disabilities, even though "everyone" talks about the importance of safety and quality? Despite expensive and sophisticated monitoring, incident reporting and quality review systems - and requirements and mandates and regulations that try to "manage" quality and safety in just about every DD agency and state across the nation?

Is it inevitable that "bad things" will happen in service systems that have become overly complex? Or, are there perhaps some basic and underlying factors that, if recognized and aggressively addressed, could make a difference? A big difference.

1

It has happened in other fields when there has been a concerted effort to reduce risk – for example, most recently in acute healthcare. Why can't it happen here - in the field of developmental disabilities?

Well it can! This series of books and on-line courses is designed to help do just that. By choosing to learn more about improving safety and reducing risk of harm you are demonstrating your interest and commitment to make a big difference in the quality of your supports and in the life of the people you serve. So, welcome to the Risk Management in DD series.

THE RISK MANAGEMENT IN DD SERIES

THE FULL SERIES includes six detailed on-line courses and accompanying books that provide useful tools for enhancing your ability to design and establish effective methods for reducing adverse events and improving the safety of services for people with intellectual and developmental disabilities (I/DD). The on-line courses include a number of audio-visual and interactive learning tools as well as downloadable forms and checklists, many of which can be filled out on-line. The accompanying books are useful as stand-alone resources or can be used to supplement the on-line experience.

All of the courses and books in this series have been specially designed to provide practical knowledge and skills for a broad range of personnel in the field of intellectual and developmental disability services (I/DD). This includes individuals who are responsible for conducting activities such as individual support planning, the coordination and supervision of services and supports, and/or the monitoring and oversight of programs and service systems that support people with I/DD in service provider and public/state systems of support and oversight. All of the books and courses include practical tools that you can use right away, including interactive forms, checklists and resources. Taken together the series represents a comprehensive risk management "toolbox" that can be used to reduce risk of harm and improve the safety and quality of services and supports to individuals who have a disability. The full series includes:

1. **MORTALITY REVIEW AND REPORTING IN DEVELOPMENTAL DISABILITIES: How to Use Mortality Review and Reporting as a Quality Enhancement Tool.** The Mortality Review and Reporting in DD resource provides information about methods for conducting mortality reviews within organizations and public agencies that serve persons with developmental disabilities. Methods for establishing review processes and analyzing and reporting findings are highlighted that are consistent with generally accepted standards for mortality review. Content includes step by step directions along with a variety of forms and checklists for setting up, managing and reporting on your mortality review process, including major findings. Information regarding simple methods to analyze mortality data and establish comparative benchmarks and improvement goals are presented.

2. **RISK SCREENING IN DEVELOPMENTAL DISABILITIES: How to Use Risk Screening to Enhance Individual Support Planning.** The Risk Screening in I/DD resource provides information on and skill development directed toward understanding some of the most important issues that pose special risks for persons with I/DD. It guides the development and design of protocols for screening risks and integrating results into individualized support plans.

Issues associated with special considerations for addressing planning needs for self-directed support models are included.

3. **ROOT CAUSE ANALYSIS IN DEVELOPMENTAL DISABILITIES: How to Use Root Cause Analysis to Prevent Adverse Events.** The Root Cause Analysis in DD resource provides introductory information on managing risk and enhancing safety in programs that serve people with I/DD. It includes step-by-step instructions for using the process of root cause analysis in the field of I/DD. Worksheets, checklists and other tools you can use are included.

4. **FAILURE MODE AND EFFECTS ANALYSIS IN DEVELOPMENTAL DISABILITIES: How to Use FMEA to Promote Safety.** The Failure Mode and Effects Analysis in DD resource provides background information and practical step-by-step instructions for using failure mode and effects analysis (FMEA) as a risk prevention tool in programs serving individuals with developmental disabilities. FMEA is a recognized method for conducting prospective review of complex processes and activities in order to identify and correct steps that have a perceived high risk of error. In this series the FMEA process is adapted to the types of issues and adverse events most common within programs and settings serving persons with developmental disabilities. Forms and other tools are included in the material along with practical examples from I/DD programs you can use to better understand how to introduce FMEA to your service system.

5. **USING DATA AS A QUALITY TOOL IN DEVELOPMENTAL DISABILITIES: How to Use Data to Promote Quality Improvement.** The Data Analysis for Quality Improvement course and associated book is designed to provide basic skills in analyzing risk and quality improvement related data. The focus of instruction is on using descriptive and inferential statistical procedures to help identify patterns and trends that may be associated with increased risk of harm, including client characteristics and environmental variables. Practical examples, templates and resources are included.

6. **INCIDENT MANAGEMENT IN DEVELOPMENTAL DISABILITIES: How to Use Information and Data as an Incident Prevention Tool.** The Incident Management in DD resource provides information on standards for establishing and enhancing existing incident reporting, review and management systems for I/DD agencies. Material includes a review of the most common incident categories that are typically present in incident management systems, methods to evaluate the usability, comprehensiveness and potential effectiveness of incident reporting systems and instruction on how to integrate findings into a more holistic risk management system. This includes the development of "triggers" for highlighting high risk situations. Checklists and other practical tools are presented.

An additional book supplement is available that is entitled **SYSTEMS DESIGN IN DEVELOPMENTAL DISABILITIES: How to Use a Comprehensive System for Risk Management.** This supplement provides information on how to "pull together" all of the various risk management tools to design a more comprehensive systems approach to safety and quality improvement in the field of intellectual and developmental disabilities. This additional material is included in each of the on-line courses and as a supplement for the books in the series. Readers interested in designing and evaluating their overall approach to risk management are encouraged to review this supplemental material.

To access the full suite of on-line courses in this series
visit the following internet site:

http://www.udiscovering.org/

and select the link for

Risk Management in Developmental Disabilities

CHAPTER 2

Getting Started:
Create a Meaningful Culture of Safety

THE FOUNDATION FOR ENHANCING SAFETY in any I/DD organization requires the presence of an organizational culture that expects everyone to focus on safe practices and promote quality in every single aspect of their work. Assuring the presence of such a vibrant organizational culture of safety is the single most important component of any risk management system. Without this foundation, efforts to ensure safety and minimize unnecessary risk to the people that are supported by an organization will be severely compromised if not impossible to achieve. Pay careful attention to it!

A culture of safety requires a strong commitment on the part of every person within the organization to think differently about safety. Beginning with senior leadership and extending outward to all stakeholders, a clear and consistent vision must be firmly embraced that represents a different "way of doing business." Direct support personnel, service providers and recipients, family members, supervisors, managers, advisory boards - literally everyone involved in the organization must see safety as essential to the delivery of quality services. They must incorporate safe practices into all of their daily activities. All members of the organization must believe that safety is essential and that they can each play an important role in making it happen – all the time. It is this organizational commitment and belief, embodied in the attitudes and behavior of its members that is meant by the concept culture of safety. Such an organizational culture is the single most important aspect for building a strong foundation for safety and quality.

A SAFE AND INFORMED CULTURE IS CRITICAL. The British psychologist James Reason[1] has addressed the importance of creating a *safe culture* by focusing on understanding important barriers that inhibit safe practices and that can interfere with the establishment of an organization-wide culture of safety. First and foremost Reason emphasizes that "an informed culture is a safe culture."[2] He notes that such a culture is embodied by a belief in the importance of a *systems* approach that continually gathers and analyzes information. A systems approach actively seeks out information that can help identify weaknesses in the system that can lead to harm - and areas where safety nets and policies are working as intended. According to Reason, an organization that has an informed and safe culture seeks constant, informed improvement and establishes an atmosphere where people are comfortable sharing mishaps and mistakes. In such an organization staff know that their leadership recognizes that most people do not deliberately try to cause harm. The members of such an organization believe that it is only through open and honest reporting and tough analysis that the real *causes* of risks can be understood and effective changes can then be made to improve safety.

5

David Marx[3] has expanded on this idea by introducing the construct of a *just culture*. In a just culture, there is a sense of fairness and openness. Managers in a just culture do not automatically blame people for mistakes, but rather look to use adverse events as learning opportunities. They seek to manage choices and redesign systems to reduce the likelihood of human error. In an organization with a just culture consequences for harmful incidents are based on an understanding of why errors may have taken place. The focus is therefore on understanding, not blaming.

Marx identifies three basic causes of adverse events that should be recognized and then addressed differently to improve the safety of the tasks and activities that are typically performed by personnel.

1. **Human error**, which is not intentional and is due to a mistake, a slip or a lapse;

2. **At-risk behavior**, which is intentional but is due to a lack of awareness of the risk, or, is due to a belief that the risk was justified in order to achieve a desired outcome; and,

3. **Reckless behavior**, which is a conscious and deliberate disregard for the risks involved.

As suggested by Marx, it is extremely important to understand the difference between these three causes of adverse events and to establish different methods of remediation and correction based on the actual cause. Unfortunately, the typical management response – using discipline and punitive consequences – may be appropriate for adverse events known to be due to reckless behavior, but it is counterproductive when such incidents are caused by actions that are unintentional (error) or where the risk was not recognized. In these instances different responses and solutions are needed.

MISTAKES HAPPEN. Sometimes people make mistakes. But when a genuine culture of safety is present within an organization, there is a shared understanding that everyone can and sometimes does make a mistake. In fact, both Marx and Reason recognize that mistakes can be valuable "lessons" and opportunities for improvement. In the health care field, it is becoming more and more recognized that "bad systems and not bad people lead to most errors."[4] This important notion is illustrated in a quote by Donald Norman[5] that is shared by Marx:

> *People make errors, which lead to accidents. Accidents lead to deaths. The standard solution is to blame the people involved. If we find out who made the errors and punish them, we solve the problem, right? Wrong. The problem is seldom the fault of an individual; it is the fault of the system. Change the people without changing the system and the problems will continue.*

Recognition of the importance of an organizational culture of safety is as important in I/DD as it is in health care and virtually every other field of endeavor. Establishing such a culture is the very first step – and an essential ingredient - for safe services that can meet the highest standards of quality in the field of I/DD.

HOW TO CREATE A STRONGER CULTURE OF SAFETY

HOW CAN YOU PROMOTE a stronger culture of safety within an I/DD organization? One of the most important first steps is to assess the organizational culture that currently exists in the organization. Think about what steps can be taken, on both a short term and longer term basis, to help establish a more positive and safe culture. You can use the checklist in **Appendix A** to guide such an evaluation and planning process. Involve others in the assessment.

Next, explore the extent to which the organization embodies important principles and practices that promote a meaningful culture of safety. Remember that effective and meaningful management of risk requires the involvement of everyone within a service organization. Pay special attention to the following practices.

STOP BLAMING. An I/DD organization with a true culture of safety creates a climate of support where staff are not fearful of retribution or punishment if they make an honest mistake or identify a problem. Rather, they feel supported by their managers and leadership within the organization to correct problems and point out issues that may jeopardize the health and safety of the people they serve - and of one another. A fear of punishment and retaliation is a powerful barrier to identifying and reporting adverse events and errors. When an atmosphere of distrust and fear is present, it is difficult if not impossible to establish an effective culture of safety. Therefore stress the need to change attitudes and beliefs (especially for managers and supervisors) and move away from "blaming" and toward "understanding." The organizational climate has to become one that encourages identification of issues in order to ascertain what needs to be changed and improved rather than focusing on who is to blame.

MAKE REPORTING CONFIDENTIAL. Experts in the field of safety (e.g., Reason) believe that open reporting can be better established when an organization sets up processes that maintain the confidentiality or "de-identification of reporters." They suggest that it is better to establish separation within the agency (or part of the agency) so that the entity that collects incident reports is different from the agency (or part of the agency) that handles discipline.

INVOLVE EVERYONE. An organization that is truly committed to safety seeks out and reinforces the active involvement of front-line staff and service recipients. It works hard to facilitate honest and open communication between staff, persons receiving supports, their families and advocates, and the leadership of the organization. Such an organization recognizes that the people closest to the problem are very often in the best position to identify it and provide practical solutions.

BE A LEARNING ORGANIZATION. In order to establish a culture that rewards safety it is important to promote constant learning. To do this, leaders should strive to make their agency a "learning organization" – one that uses information from outside their immediate system to better understand the causes of adverse events and potential solutions to problems. In other words, work to become an organization that actively seeks the experiences of other industries and other agencies to help target processes and systems that can be improved. As noted by some experts (e.g., Marx), an adverse event should not be seen as simply something to be fixed, but also something to learn from. An organization that has a firm foundation of safety doesn't let "good enough be good enough," but rather it consistently seeks opportunities to gather information for improvement - from all stakeholders - at all levels of the organization – and especially from outside of the organization.

STRIVE TO UNDERSTAND WHY. Perhaps most importantly, an organization with a well-established culture of safety always attempts to look beyond "fault" and tries to understand <u>why</u> an error took place. This drive for understanding is essential. It represents a mind-set that is deeply engrained in the organization and shared by everyone. It is a belief that we must understand not only what happened, but why it happened. Only then can an effective plan for lasting change become a reality. Such an organization moves beyond a focus on blame and punishment - which addresses only the immediate event. An organization with a functioning culture of safety strives to implement systemic change - improvements in procedures and protocols - in how business is done. In other words, it seeks changes and improvements that can actually reduce the risk of harm to the people it supports and to bring about long-term positive change; not simply implement changes that "look good."

UNDERSTAND THE ROLE OF HUMAN ERROR

RECOGNIZING THE CRITICAL ROLE OF HUMAN ERROR in causing adverse events is necessary for creating a safe environment for people with disabilities. Almost all services and supports that are provided to persons with intellectual or developmental disabilities are labor intensive, i.e., they require people – usually staff, volunteers or family members – to conduct a task or activity with and on behalf of the person with the disability. Sometimes these tasks are rather complex and therefore prone to errors. Before effective risk prevention strategies can be established, it is necessary to identify what type of error led to an adverse event. Efforts to correct problems or prevent future incidents will fail if there is not an understanding of why something went wrong. The enhancement of safety, management of risk and promotion of quality demand that you and your organizational leadership recognize and understand the role of human error.

DIFFERENTIATE THE DIFFERENT KINDS OF HUMAN ERRORS. As noted above, it is important to recognize that not all human errors are the same. For example, Patricia Spath[6] has categorized errors that take place in health care settings such as hospitals using a classification that can be readily applied to I/DD services. A simple adaptation to this method for categorizing errors results in a classification of errors as either *active* or *latent*. When you go about analyzing adverse events and the potential for risk of harm to people in your program and/or service think carefully these two major types of errors and how they have contributed to the incident under study.

ACTIVE ERRORS are human errors that are usually committed by a person or group of people, most often front-line direct support personnel who are working with the individual with a disability. These types of error are the most "noticeable" and are usually associated with the proximate cause of an adverse event, i.e., they take place immediately before the incident. There are three major types of active errors that can take place:

- **Slips** – these are *unintentional deviations* from an established procedure, often due to distraction or inadequate attention to the task at hand. Very often the person making the error forgets to do something or does it at the wrong time. For example, consider a staff member who, while preparing an individual for transfer using a mechanical lift, is interrupted and asked a series of questions about how to conduct the program for another person. The staff member fails to properly attach the restraining strap on the first person who subsequently falls and injures himself.

- **Mistakes** – these are often due to *faulty reasoning* and *poor judgment*. They are not intentional and are often associated with a novel or new situation or even when supporting an individual the staff member may not be familiar with. Mistakes that take place when performing a more complex activity have a high probability of resulting in an adverse event. For example, consider the situation where a staff member is directed to supervise an individual they have never supported before due to the regular person calling in sick. The new staff member provides the individual with paper materials that are part of an activity they often conduct with other service recipients. However, the new staff member is not aware that the consumer has a history of impulsive behavior and pica. The service recipient tears the paper and begins to ingest it, and then begins to choke. This was a mistake (not intentional) related to lack of familiarity with the person they were supporting.

- **Unsafe practices** – these errors are associated with an *intentional* or *conscious decision* to do something "risky." Unsafe practices are almost always a direct violation of rules and/or standards. They often take place when a staff member is "rushed" or makes a deliberate decision to take a "short cut" in order to save time or make a difficult task easier. Sometimes the unsafe practice can even take place as a function of staff convenience. For example, consider this: a staff member leaves a person temporarily alone in a van in order to "run into a store" because there is no parking nearby and getting the service recipient to cooperate with exiting and entering the van will take a lot of time and effort. The staff member is aware that the individual has a history of running away when unsupervised, but they decide that the risk is "worth it" since they will be gone only for a few minutes. When the staff member is in the store, the service recipient leaves the van and runs into the street where she is hit by a car. The intentional act by the staff member led to the adverse incident.

LATENT FAULTS are errors or faults in *system design* that serve to set the stage for active errors. They are usually the responsibility of management. Latent faults increase the probability that a slip, mistake or unsafe practice will occur at some time in the future. Latent faults usually have the following characteristics:

- **Delayed impact** – the fault or system design failure is usually *not immediately evident* and often goes unrecognized. It is identified only after one or more significant adverse events have taken place that result in an analysis of the system as a whole.

- **Set the stage for failure** – latent faults are most often present early in the "chain of events" that leads up to an adverse event. They *set the stage* for later errors by staff. Latent faults are often associated with confusing policy and procedure, inadequate training, scheduling issues (e.g., multiple activities at the same time) or staff

9

shortages, punitive work environments that lead to stress, and fear of failure, and conflicting priorities and unrealistic expectations.

A careful analysis of the most serious adverse events will be able to identify the presence of BOTH active errors and latent faults. Whenever you are designing a program, developing an individual support plan, reviewing protocols or conducting a retrospective or prospective hazard analysis make sure you consider the entire "chain" of possible events that could cause an adverse event to take place. Work backwards from the most obvious or proximate cause of the incident to uncover those system design factors that set the stage for active errors by staff. A failure to do this will most likely result in an incomplete understanding of what led up to and therefore contributed to the adverse event. This will result in you "solving" the wrong problem and thus increase the probability that in the future the same type of adverse event will take place.

REVIEW THE ENTIRE ERROR CHAIN. A more complete understanding of what has caused and/or contributed to an adverse event therefore requires you to carefully review the full sequence of events that preceded the incident. All too often only the actions and errors associated with direct support personnel are reviewed during incident investigations. This results in a tendency to focus on "corrective" actions such as retraining and staff discipline that will not address the underlying problem that led to the human error in the first place. Meaningful corrective actions will only take place when management makes an effort to identify latent faults in the system that set the stage for staff errors. If a particular type of adverse event occurs over and over again, it is imperative that you take the time to carefully review the entire error chain. Effective management of risk can only <u>prevent</u> future incidents when it targets underlying systems faults

Typical Error Chain
in I/DD Services

Management		Front line Staff	

LATENT FAULT → Activity or Task → ACTIVE ERROR → Intervening Actions → Proximate Cause → ADVERSE EVENT

System design factor that sets the stage for active errors:
- Erroneous management decision – bad design of system
- Inadequate staffing or training
- Confusing policy or overly technical protocol
- Poor supervison and support

Error by a person resulting in an unsafe practice:
- Slip
- Mistake
- Deviation

Most immediate cause of harm:
- Commissions
- Omissions

PROGRAM VARIABLES THAT INCREASE ERROR.

THERE ARE A NUMBER of important and somewhat unique characteristics of services and supports to individuals with an intellectual and/or other developmental disability that can increase the risk of error by support providers. Some of the more important risk factors that can promote error in the I/DD field include:

1. **VARIABILITY.** The risk of human error is directly related to the degree of variability or the difference in the needs and characteristics of the people being served and the people who provide the support. It is also related to differences that exist in the routines, activities and types of settings within which those supports are provided. The greater the variability, the greater the risk an error will occur.

   a. **People.** Unlike many other service organizations and industries, the people served by I/DD systems typically span a very broad range of capabilities and therefore have substantial variability in individual needs and preferences. This broad difference in needs and preferences requires the introduction of highly individualized and unique services. Such "people variability" is present due to a wide range of:

      i. Physical capabilities and physical disabilities

      ii. Intellectual capacity

      iii. Behavioral health and challenges and the need for unique behavior support and intervention plans

      iv. Medical co-morbidities and the need for specialized health-related care

   b. **Staff.** Unlike medical services and acute healthcare (as well as many other professional service industries) there are currently no recognized national credentialing, standards or professional criteria for direct support personnel in the field of I/DD in the United States. Therefore, it is not unusual for the individuals who provide care and support to persons with disabilities to also exhibit significant variability in their skills and ability to deliver consistent and often complicated care related services. This is especially true now that self-directed support using person-selected support assistants has become more widely utilized. Such staff variability is illustrated by differences in staff:

      i. Educational background and training

      ii. Knowledge and experience

      iii. Skills and competency

      iv. Language proficiencies and culture

   c. **Services.** Given the wide range of needs within the population typically served by most I/DD programs, the types of services and individualized supports that are provided vary significantly, and cover a very expansive range, including supports related to:

      i. Residential living

11

    ii.   Special education and employment

    iii.   Community access and leisure activities

    iv.   Transportation

    v.   Health care and nursing related care

    vi.   Behavior management

    vii.   Physical mobility, communication and adapted technology

Even within any given category of support there is even greater variability (e.g., supervised living, independent living, group homes, foster care, institutional care, etc. just for the one category referred to as *residential* living). The same types of differences exist in all of the other major support and service categories. Such variability is essential for assuring there is a focus on individualized supports that can better meet personal needs and preferences. But, with such variability comes increased risk of human error that should be recognized when designing systems of support.

2.   **COMPLEXITY.** The more complex a task or activity, the higher the risk of error. The delivery of services in the field of I/DD has become increasingly more complex over the years. The sophistication and complexity of the activities staff are called upon to perform raises the probability that errors will be made. This important relationship between task complexity and error has been studied more extensively in the field of healthcare than in the field of I/DD. However, since many of the issues between the two fields of practice are extremely similar, we can extrapolate many of the findings and projections. For instance, The Institute for Healthcare Improvement[7] suggests that the number of steps in any activity performed by healthcare workers – despite the inherent reliability of each individual step - is directly related to the probability an error will occur. For example, if a task has 25 steps, and the reliability of each step is 99%, the task will be completed without any error only 78% of the time. This means that there is a 22% chance an error will occur each time the activity or task is undertaken! Many of the individual programs and the tasks that staff are called upon to conduct with persons who have more significant disabilities have at least 25 to 50 separate steps. Many tasks have steps that must be performed in a particular sequence and in response to subtle cues and individual reactions of the person receiving support. This translates into a relatively high probability that errors will occur.

It is therefore highly likely that some type of human error will take place in most complex processes or activities performed by staff who work in I/DD services. Fortunately however, most errors do not necessarily lead to serious adverse events – at least not to incidents that cause severe harm. Unfortunately, many of the tasks that direct support personnel serving people with severe disabilities are asked to perform on a regular basis are extremely complex. Consequently they are therefore very prone to errors taking place. Those errors can – over time - have very negative consequences, including severe injury and sometimes even accidental death. Just think about the total number of complex tasks that are performed every day in your organization and you can begin to recognize that the potential for human error is enormous.

Consider the following examples of complex activities that are typically performed in I/DD programs that are prone to increased risk of error and resultant injury or death:

- **Mealtime and eating.** Preparing special diets and implementing specialized feeding programs for persons with significant swallowing disorders.

- **Behavior.** Implementing complex behavior management programs, sometimes including the use of physical contact and restraint, with persons who are resistive, confused and aggressive.

- **Medication.** Administering multiple medications, some of which are extremely potent and must be maintained within a relatively narrow therapeutic range.

- **Bathing.** Assuring that persons with very limited muscle control are safe and comfortable when participating in special bathing procedures.

- **Transportation.** Properly implementing lift and transfer protocols for persons with mobility disabilities and providing proper support and management of persons at risk of aggressive behavior and/or running when being transported.

3. **COUPLING.** Coupling is a concept that refers to the extent to which discrete steps in an activity follow each other in rapid succession. The less time there is between steps, the greater the degree of coupling. Tightly coupled tasks are associated with increased error since there is little, if any time to recognize mistakes and take corrective action before the next step in the activity must be implemented. Tightly coupled tasks are therefore more prone to progressive errors. For example, if a particular step is not performed correctly it may become difficult, if not impossible, to perform the next step correctly. If there is no time delay between these steps, the errors cascade (i.e., one error quickly contributes to the next and to the next, and so on). This error progression provides little or no opportunity to stop or interrupt the process in time to prevent harm from taking place.

There are many different types of "tightly coupled" tasks or activities in I/DD programs. A few of the more common activities include:

a. **Restraint.** When staff implement a physical restraint or other physical management technique with an individual who is highly agitated it can require very fast responses on the part of the staff, with little time to "think through" or correct minor mistakes in how they are applying the restraint and responding to the person. This can quickly lead to mistakes and resulting injury to the individual and even the staff.

b. **Feeding.** Providing food and nourishment to an individual who has a significant swallowing disorder and who may be restless and/or resistant (e.g., moving and shaking their head) can often require quick reactions on the part of staff as they move through the sequential steps of the feeding procedure. Even minor errors in feeding someone with a swallowing disorder can lead to choking and the potential for aspiration.

c. **Lift and transfer.** Assisting an individual with limited motor control very often requires almost instantaneous responses and corrective reactions on the part of staff, particularly if the individual resists physical support. The lack of time between sequential steps in this type of activity can lead to progressive errors that can result in "accidental" falls and severe injury.

4. **LIMITED STANDARDIZATION.** Standardization usually increases the probability that certain tasks or activities will be performed the same way, every time and by every staff person. Such standardization reduces error and the resultant risk of an adverse event. That is why many industries (e.g., aviation, nuclear engineering, industrial manufacturing, and medical surgery) spend significant time and resources on evaluating procedures and developing formal protocols that require the use of standardized procedures and formal checklists that must be strictly adhered to by personnel.

The movement in the field of I/DD toward "individualization" and "person-centered" approaches to care and support that reflect personal preferences and needs has undoubtedly promoted great improvement in the quality of life and quality of service for the persons with disabilities. These trends have also made it more difficult to standardize programs, services, procedures and the myriad tasks that staff are asked to perform every day. Consequently, those who are responsible for designing and managing programs and services must recognize that many care and support procedures will not be conducted the same way every time they are carried out by staff and therefore more prone to human error.

In addition to the "individual" focus present within I/DD services, a number of other factors may also operate to reduce the standardization of procedures. Some of these include:

- **Lack of familiarity with people and routines.** Long term retention of direct support professionals is a special challenge for many service providers due to the demands of the work and pay and benefits that may not be competitive. This can lead to frequent turnover of personnel. Staffing requirements can also lead to personnel being "pulled" from one program setting to another to ensure adequate coverage. Both of these factors tend to compromise the ability of staff to become familiar with the individual needs and communication styles of the people they support and the special (and often complicated) individualized programs that must be provided to each individual. This lack of familiarity with people and routines can heighten the risk for mistakes and errors that can cause harm.

- **Multiple providers.** Different service providers may be present for an individual's residential versus employment related supports. Different service providers often have different methods and procedures, not to mention different support staff that interact with individuals with a disability. This makes standardization of tasks and activities extremely difficult if not impossible across providers, even when specific protocols are present. The result is an increased risk of human error.

- **Dispersed services.** The I/DD service system has made remarkable progress in helping people live and work within a more integrated and community-based support system. People live semi-independently or in very small group residences. They work in individualized jobs with varying degrees of intermittent support. This major change in how services are delivered has resulted in a highly distributed support system where staff often work alone or with a very small number of colleagues. The presence of direct supervision and direction is often not available. The reduction in direct supervision and the limited presence of other staff to answer questions, discover mistakes before they cause any harm, and provide assistance can increase the risk of error. In addition, programs and service settings may, even for a single provider, be quite geographically distant from one another, resulting in differences in supervision and management expectations and methods. Certainly this doesn't mean small settings and independent supports should be eliminated. Far too much good has accrued from these changes to the service system. It does suggest however that leadership must be aware of the potential for increased risk when assigning staff and establishing methods for training personnel and providing supervision and technical assistance to staff. Dispersed supports may increase the probability of human error; therefore this increase in risk needs to be accounted for.

- **Technical programs.** Many person-specific programs and support plans are extremely complex and written in technical and "dense" language that results in staff interpretation errors (e.g., "winging it") that can differ from what the clinician expected. The more technical and complex a procedure, the greater the risk of human error. When possible, simplify protocols and use plain language to describe what staff needs to do.

- **Lack of training and supervision.** Very often there is a relative dearth of direct "hands-on" training, practice and supervisory oversight associated with support plans and complex procedures in I/DD settings. Personnel are expected to understand exactly how to perform tasks, even when they may be novel or complicated. Inadequate training and direct supervision can lead to substantial variation in how a procedure is actually implemented. This variation only serves to increase the probability of human error and the potential for an adverse event.

5. **DEPENDENCE ON PEOPLE.** The delivery of support and services to persons with I/DD is a very "labor intensive" business that is almost exclusively dependent upon people (staff and personal assistants) doing something for or with an individual. Unfortunately, people make mistakes! Activities and processes that are dependent upon people are therefore quite prone to human error. It is important to recognize this simple fact. Systems must be designed with an understanding that errors and mistakes <u>will</u> take place. Support systems and programs for individuals need to be designed to avoid reliance on *errorless* performance since that simply will rarely if ever be present in the "real world." Expect that mistakes will sometimes happen and build in methods to reduce the probability and/or the impact of those mistakes. [Note: the risk management procedure called Failure Mode Effects and Analysis is designed to do that. Interested readers may wish to explore this tool in greater detail.]

6. **INADEQUATE TIME.** When staff do not have enough time to properly complete tasks they often end up "rushing" and using shortcuts. This in turn can result in staff "unofficially" altering protocols and written procedures in order to "get it done" on time. When this happens the steps in complex tasks become more tightly coupled and completed more quickly without providing time to address problems or errors that take place in the previous steps of a procedure. When staff are rushing they tend to feel overwhelmed and anxious. This associated stress can increase the probability of mistakes and errors.

It is not uncommon in many I/DD programs for far too many specific activities and tasks to be scheduled in a very compressed time period. This is particularly true within formal residential programs, especially during the morning and early evening. During these periods many competing tasks must be completed in a limited amount of time. All too often performance evaluations are based on whether or not staff complete required tasks in the allotted time, not on whether the tasks and activities are actually conducted in a safe fashion. Program managers should therefore carefully evaluate what they expect to be performed and whether or not the amount of allotted time is sufficient for required activities to be safely conducted. They should also think carefully about the unintended consequences of management expectations (e.g., quantity and timeliness versus safety of staff actions).

7. **DISTRACTION.** It is not unusual for residential, employment/day, recreation and even transportation services and program settings to be confusing environments that contain multiple visual distractions, are loud and noisy (many people talking at once), and have different individuals vying for attention all at the same time. Such distraction can easily serve to divert the attention of staff as they attempt to complete complex procedures or implement a highly technical program or task. This can lead to the potential for mistakes and errors that can result in an adverse event, sometimes one that causes injury or harm to an individual. A few examples of distractions could include any of the following:

   - The phone rings when a staff member in a residence is preparing a special diet. She forgets exactly what to do next;

   - Another individual interrupts and asks a question of a staff member when preparing medications for distribution and administration. He miss counts and fails to provide all the necessary medications;

   - Two individuals become agitated and begin arguing with one another. This leads to a staff member temporarily leaving another person unattended whom they were assisting prepare a meal on the stove. This person burns their hand on the stove.

PEOPLE CHARACTERISTICS THAT CAN INCREASE ERROR. In addition to program and setting factors that can increase risk of human error, there are some special characteristics of the people who are supported in I/DD programs that can pose especially high risk and should therefore always be carefully reviewed to enhance safety and improve quality within your organization. Some of these more important "people" characteristics include:

1. **IMPULSIVE BEHAVIOR.** Individuals with impulsive behavior require especially vigilant supervision since they are often "driven" to engage in potentially harmful behaviors. Very brief periods of inattention can sometimes result in opportunities for the impulsive behavior to manifest itself. Some common examples of risk associated with impulsive behavior include:

   a. Impulsive food ingestion, including pica

   b. Self-injury

   c. Aggression towards other people

    d.   Sexual offending

    e.   Running away from required supervision (e.g., AWOL)

2. **INJURIES AND ILLNESS.** The presence of injuries and/or illness in persons with limited communication skills sometimes makes it very difficult to correctly identify and diagnose a potential problem that may require timely intervention. Consequently, injuries and serious illnesses can sometimes go unrecognized until they have progressed and result in observable signs or have become extremely painful or debilitating.

3. **LIMITED MOTOR CONTROL.** Individuals who have significant physical disabilities are at an increased risk of harm in activities that require motor control. Lifting and transfer, bathing, transportation, sleeping and other types of activities where the absence of an ability to stand, sit, roll over and exercise trunk control can pose special risks. A very special concern that should always be considered is the risk of falls in this group of people.

4. **MEDICATIONS.** Individuals with I/DD often receive relatively complex medication regimens that require very careful administration and close observation for harmful side effects. It is not unusual for some individuals to have a variety of different health care providers, each of whom prescribes medication, and sometimes without the timely awareness of the other medications a person is receiving. In addition, many individuals with I/DD receive potent psychotropic medications that can have relatively serious side effects if not adequately monitored. These situations, along with the prescription of drugs that must be maintained within a very narrow therapeutic range, place certain individuals with I/DD at heightened risk of harm.

5. **SPECIAL DIETS.** A number of persons who have very severe intellectual and physical disabilities receive special diets that can involve the need for specific and careful preparation of foods along with the implementation of highly individualized feeding protocols. The presence of a swallowing disorder makes this group of individuals extremely vulnerable to choking and aspiration.

6. **COMMUNICATION SKILLS.** Many of the people who receive support in I/DD programs may have limited communication skills, particularly the inability to use verbal communication. Some people have difficulty communicating to staff and others when they are experiencing distress, pain, anxiety, anger or confusion. The absence of good verbal communication skills requires staff and others who provide support to be especially vigilant in picking up on and properly interpreting non-verbal signs. This requires knowledge of the person and careful attention to body language and overt behaviors that may be a sign that something is wrong and that immediate assistance is needed. Very often these non-verbal cues are unique to each person and require experience and familiarity with the individual to be properly interpreted.

7. **INDIVIDUALIZED SUPPORT PLANS.** Certainly one of the most important aspects of providing meaningful and effective support to people with developmental disabilities is the use of very personalized and highly individualized support plans. This greatly improves the quality and appropriateness of supports. However, with that benefit has come an increase in risk of error that simply must be recognized and addressed. As noted earlier, a common method in many other industries for increasing safety and reducing the probability of error is to focus on

standardization of tasks and activities – in other words, a procedure is performed exactly the same way every time, by everyone. The use of individualized programs means that tasks and activities are not designed using a "cookie cutter" approach. Therefore, staff are required to remember many different ways of providing a similar service or support that is tailored to an individual service recipient and his or her unique needs and preferences. This difference in "how something is done" inevitably introduces a risk of error. This doesn't mean individualized service and support planning should be discontinued. That would be a travesty and negatively impact on the quality of life for persons with a disability. It simply means supervisors, program authors and managers in I/DD services organizations and systems need to be cognizant of this risk factor and continually put in place environmental cues, practical training and enhanced methods of supervision. They must also establish a true culture of safety and involve all stakeholders in the evaluation of the safety of services and supports on continual basis.

SPECIAL CONCERNS IN SELF DIRECTED SUPPORTS

MORE AND MORE I/DD service systems are embracing self-directed supports as a means of expanding choice and control by individuals and their families over what services they receive, who provides personal support and how that support is to be provided. This approach can greatly enrich the quality of life for individuals with disabilities. However, it can also bring with it a variety of unique risks that should be recognized and then addressed by the service system. In addition to the more common issues that can lead to adverse events and that are typically present within the more traditional service system, a variety of additional risks can sometimes present themselves for persons relying on self-directed supports.

Some of these additional risks that may be present in self-directed support and should therefore be taken into consideration include:

1. Hiring and retaining sufficient individuals to provide needed support;

2. Assuring proper background checks of support personnel;

3. Training of and developing critical skills for those who provide support;

4. Establishing backup systems to ensure support staff are available when scheduled and needed; and

5. Monitoring for and properly reviewing and investigating incidents of abuse and neglect

Systematic and easy to use methods for providing individuals with simple tools to help them manage the supports they receive are essential. It is equally important to make sure the individual and his/her circle of support and/or family has access to practical risk mitigation tools. Thus, the focus for those who design, manage and oversee I/DD services and supports needs to focus to a much greater extent on supporting the individual with the disability safely manage their own supports.

ENHANCE QUALITY AND SAFETY BY MANAGING RISK EFFECTIVELY

ENHANCING SAFETY and promoting quality requires that all I/DD support organizations and service systems work hard to establish a robust and meaningful culture of safety. To do this they must continually work to develop and actively use analytic tools to identify problems and guide actions for preventing adverse events.

Some of these tools are presented in the books and on-line courses that are included in the **Risk Management in DD** series. As noted, the series is designed to help interested support personnel, managers, clinicians and other stakeholders apply practical approaches to risk mitigation and safety enhancement – tools that are tailored to the special issues and needs present in service programs and public and private systems that support people with intellectual and developmental disabilities.

Remember, analytic approaches to safety and quality and the use of techniques such as those presented throughout this series (e.g., root cause analysis, risk screening, mortality review, failure mode effects analysis, and incident management) – however, are just tools. They must be used properly by people who are skilled and trained. For these tools to be most effective, all the people within your organization must really believe that safety is important and that better quality in services is achievable. You can help them achieve this.

Bad things may happen to people with disabilities, but remember that you and your colleagues can make a big difference in reducing harmful events and increasing opportunities for individuals with a disability to experience a true quality of life. Continue your study by moving on to the next chapter; and then, to additional resources in the **Risk Management in DD** series.

CHAPTER 3
The Utility of Data

THERE IS A GROWING RECOGNITION across almost all fields of endeavor – business, health care, education and government – that objective measurement and analysis of performance can be a powerful management tool. Such objective assessment requires data. While there are many pitfalls to an overreliance on data, when combined with other approaches to assessment, it can provide an excellent means of identifying where change may be needed in a service system that supports people with intellectual and developmental disabilities (I/DD). The proper use of data can also help to identify what type of change may be the most helpful.

None other than Bill Gates, the co-founder of the technology giant Microsoft and a respected business leader and philanthropist, has emphasized the central role of data and the use of measurement systems for solving major problems that confront the world today. As noted by Mr. Gates, "*From the fight against polio to fixing education, what's missing is often good measurement and a commitment to following the data. We can do better. We have tools at hand.*"[1] In the field of I/DD we have a great deal of data (so much in fact that it can often seem overwhelming). As suggested by Gates, we too can make better use of that data. As will be reviewed in this course, we too have many of the "tools at hand" necessary to promote safety and meaningful improvement in the services and supports that we provide to persons with disabilities.

Historically, developmental disabilities (DD) service systems have relied upon more anecdotal information (e.g., individual cases, problems in a program) to identify risks and guide change. While valuable, such an approach is open to significant bias as it is based upon personal experience and often isolated incidents. Anecdote does not always tell the "whole story" or provide a complete "picture" of what is and is not happening to people and within our service settings. The use of data – if properly analyzed and evaluated – can overcome many of these limitations. It is usually more objective and not as strongly influenced by personal bias. It allows information to be better standardized and therefore comparable across groups of people or service providers. Most importantly it can be organized and analyzed so that we can learn about change, trends, patterns and relationships.

To use data effectively requires that users have a basic understanding of the benefits and limitations of their data. It is important to keep in mind that data may be able to provide answers to some questions, but a single source of data may not provide a complete understanding when reviewed in isolation. Often initial data findings lead to more probative questions, and different types of information may be necessary in order to develop a complete understanding of an issue, problems and solutions within the service system.

THE 5 W'S

WHEN ATTEMPTING TO UNDERSTAND an event or series of events that have impacted an individual or group of people (e.g., an adverse event) it is useful to ask a series of "W" questions that can often be effectively informed by data and its proper analysis. These five "W" questions are:

- **W**HO was involved and impacted by the event
- **W**HAT exactly happened,
- **W**HEN did it take place,
- **W**HERE did it occur, and
- **W**HY did it happen (underlying causes)

THE IMPORTANCE OF ANSWERING WHY? Many types of data that are collected in the field of I/DD can directly answer the first four questions (who, what, when and where) relatively easily. However they are often not able to provide meaningful answers to the fifth question: "why" something happened. For example, data typically collected by most I/DD agencies about hospital emergency room visits usually provides a count (e.g., on a monthly basis) of (a) how many people went to the emergency room, (b) who they were, (c) when the visits took place and, (d) even at what hospital. This type of data is helpful in establishing trends and patterns, but it cannot shed much light on "why" the ER visits were needed in the first place. The answer to that last question is critical for understanding what changes in services and systems might yield the most benefit and improve the quality of health related care. Information about "why" is very often needed to effectively change protocols and policies and to drive the process of continuous and ongoing improvement to systems and the quality of services and support. It is therefore very important to recognize the limitations of any data that is being reviewed and analyzed and to pursue additional methods when and if questions regarding causality (i.e., "why") are desired.

HOW TO ANSWER THE QUESTION OF WHY? It is important to remember that the vast majority of incidents that potentially could or actually do cause harm and present significant risk to service recipients are usually not even reported. This means that there are many more "near misses" and errors that take place in I/DD services than are captured in critical incident or other formal reporting systems (see illustration on the next page). Therefore, it is not unusual for only the most obvious or serious adverse events and incidents to come to the attention of the organization and its quality and risk management systems. These serious incidents, often referred to as "sentinel events," usually demand further exploration and effort to identify and really understand "why" the incident occurred.

But, such sentinel events (i.e., incidents that result in very serious injury, harm or even avoidable death) actually represent only an extremely tiny proportion of actual incidents or potential failures and errors. They usually lead to focused investigation and may even result in the use of more demanding formal analytic tools such as Root Cause Analysis.

However, less demanding and time consuming approaches to understanding "why" an event, "near miss" or failure has taken place can and should be used on a more regular basis than may typically take place in most I/DD service organizations in order to guide corrective actions. Failure to systematically review and analyze serious and even less obvious adverse incidents can lead to haphazard action and improvement efforts, akin to "shooting in the dark" in a search for effective solutions to problems that can and do eventually cause harm.

Possible methods to explore the causes of actual and potential incidents can include: (a) apparent cause analysis[i], (b) reflective or qualitative reviews, (c) periodic discussions with front-line/direct support personnel who were actually involved in the incident/near miss, (d) "after-action" or focused debriefing interviews following an incident or observed error, and (e) statistical pattern analyses for identifying relationships between multiple variables. Such approaches can all be helpful in seeking to better understand "why" certain types of events are taking place with an individual, within a program and even across a service system or over time.

Iceberg Analogy
Continuum for Adverse Events

Only a small fraction of incidents that have resulted in actual harm are visible to the system and end up being reported - and therefore attended to. They represent the "tip of the iceberg." A far greater number of incidents and "near misses" (almost incidents) take place every day in every service setting. Human errors and process failures are even more common – with many eventually leading or contributing to an adverse event.

Special Consideration: When using data, it is extremely important to recognize which types of questions the data can realistically inform and which questions it cannot accurately answer.

---

[i] Apparent Cause Analysis (ACA) is often used in the field of engineering and power generation. It attempts to gather information that will help identify the probable causes of an incident. Since it does not typically require the exacting review process used in Root Cause Analysis (RCA), its use should be limited to those types of events that are less likely to occur or that result in less severe harm than the sentinel events selected for review by RCA.

22

BALANCE IS ESSENTIAL

JUST AS THE USE OF DATA can become a powerful tool, it can also be abused and misused. Effective risk management and quality improvement systems in I/DD organizations should strive to balance the use of data with other methods of inquiry and approaches to system improvement. An overreliance on data can just as easily hide the truth as reveal it.

Integrate and Balance Different Sources of Information

When considering the proper balance of data with other forms of information, it is critical to remember that:

- Objective data can be poorly analyzed, incorrectly interpreted and easily manipulated so that it leads to faulty conclusions.

- Data can quickly become confusing and overly complicated, resulting in users pushing it aside and falling back on old "tried and true" methods that are wrought with bias and inaccuracy. [This is often the case in the early stages of transition from paper-based to electronic systems when users can become overwhelmed with new and novel – and excessive amounts of data.]

- It is important to review data systems in order to sort through what data is useful for systemic risk mitigation and quality improvement activities and what data is not.

- Care must be taken to avoid efforts to create the "perfect" data-based review system. This can lead to valuable financial and staff resources being pulled away from other equally important activities. Such resource redirection can result in as many and perhaps even greater problems than not strengthening the data systems.

> **Special Consideration:** Data should be viewed as only one type of tool for inclusion in a comprehensive risk management and quality improvement system. It is not the "be all-end all" solution to risk management and quality improvement!

USING DATA AND THE QUALITY FRAMEWORK

MANY OF THE PROGRAMS and services used by people with I/DD are directly or indirectly funded by the federal-state Medicaid Home and Community Based Services (HCBS) waiver program. Through this program, states apply to the Centers for Medicare and Medicaid Services (CMS) for financial support of services provided outside of the regular Medicaid benefits. In order to receive this type of waiver the state must adhere to a variety of requirements regarding the safety and quality of HCBS services and the process they use for monitoring and assuring that quality. For instance, CMS requires that states operate a comprehensive quality management system. The system must assure compliance with established standards, be designed to reduce adverse events, lead to ongoing improvement, and cross all waiver programs operated by the state. CMS established a multidimensional model for designing such a quality management system referred to as the Quality Framework[2]. This framework establishes three basic functions for a quality system that are integrated with a series of focus areas. An older version of the framework that incorporates four functions is illustrated below.[ii]

QUALITY FRAMEWORK

Design function no longer included in CMS model

[ii] As noted, the current version of the Framework does not include the function of "Design" that is presented in the illustrations and discussions in this book and on-line courses in the *Risk Management in DD* series. The authors of this book and series however believe that it is important to consider the concept of "designing" quality and risk management systems so that they can readily accomplish discovery, remediation and improvement across the focus areas identified in the Framework. Consequently "Design" is included in this series.

Objective data, when organized and analyzed appropriately, can help meet CMS requirements and expectations as outlined within the Quality Framework. In doing so, it will greatly enhance an organization's efforts to identify and remediate unnecessary risk and improve the quality of services and supports that are provided to individuals with intellectual and developmental disabilities. The table below lists a few examples to illustrate how data can be useful in an I/DD service organization.

How Data can Help Meet Quality Requirements

Quality Management Function	How Data Can Help
DESIGN	In the design phase, it is important to build systems for the collection of valid and objective data about safety, quality and the performance of your service system. The use of such data allows an organization to plan methods that allow it to discover issues, remediate them and monitor their ongoing status and improvement. When redesigning quality systems, historic data can be useful as a means of guiding and informing the design process so that it can more effectively ensure risk mitigation and service quality. For example, data collection and analysis can create mechanisms that can 'trigger' early warning signs of risk of harm based on prior analysis, thus promoting timely intervention and remediation.
DISCOVER	Objective data supported by analytic processes can help answer "who," "what," when" and "where" questions. This can aid in the discovery of events that require closer examination. This data can be used to identify both successes and failures within a service system. Often this data comes from processes that continuously monitor certain events or outcomes (such as incident reporting) and can be structured to signal changes in expected patterns, promoting timely intervention.
REMEDIATE	Analytic processes can help answer "why" questions and thereby aid in the identification of the systemic issue that is contributing to events (both good and bad) and driving outcomes. It can be of assistance in targeting remedial actions that more directly lead to focused risk mitigation and quality improvement. However, other methods such as RCA, ACA, debriefing, and incident review should be used along with data analysis when designing remediation activities. The combination of these types of approaches will result in more effective and efficient outcomes.
IMPROVE	Objective data can be useful in assessing the effectiveness of remediation initiatives and in determining whether or not they are resulting in the desired improvement. When properly structured, such performance or outcome measurement is essential for driving meaningful change.

Chapter 4
Improving the Quality of Data

THE FINDINGS AND CONCLUSIONS that are drawn from the analysis of data are only as useful as the data that informs the analysis in the first place. This basic point is sometimes represented by the saying, "garbage in, garbage out." In other words, if the information that is collected within the data system is not very reliable (consistent) or valid (accurate), then the analysis of that information will be rather questionable and could lead to faulty conclusions. This could in turn result in a variety of negative consequences, ranging from a simple waste of time and resources all the way to severe adverse events that end up hurting people and the organization itself.

The system that is used to collect the data plays a very important role in determining whether the information will or will not meet recognized standards of data quality. Good information systems will help ensure that the data is:

- Reliable – i.e., it is collected the same way - each time - by all persons who input the information;

- Valid - meaning what is collected is accurate and unbiased information;

- Comprehensive - i.e., the type and amount of information that is reported is complete and sufficient to accurately answer intended questions, and

- Timely - the data and associated information is collected and reported within prescribed timelines and such that it reflects the current state of affairs.

These four fundamental standards are perhaps the most important of a series of ten basic requirements that are considered essential ingredients for data systems in I/DD organizations and that are listed below. Organizations should take sufficient time to think carefully about how well the data they rely on for risk management and quality improvement activities does or does not meet these recommended requirements. I/DD service organizations and oversight agencies should periodically evaluate the quality of their data in order to identify concerns and establish plans for systematic improvement in data quality. The checklist contained in **Appendix B** (Checklist for Assessing Your Data System) can be used to conduct such an assessment. This should be done before conducting any detailed data analyses and especially when the results of analyses appear questionable.

Although it may take time to institute major changes to large data systems and require careful preparation and training of users before implementing changes, the periodic assessment of the quality of an organization's data is well worth the time and effort. It is also critical to recognize that new technologies, changes to services and support delivery systems, feedback from users and the results of data analyses will all demand ongoing efforts to assess need for change and improvement.

10 Basic Requirements for Good Data

Standard	What it Means
RELIABILITY	Information is precise and consistent across settings, programs and reporters. Operational definitions have been established for describing variables. Periodic probes are conducted to assess the consistency of the information.
VALIDITY	Information and data are accurate and pertain to key issues under review. Data allow you to answer important questions and draw conclusions concerning the issue under review.
COMPREHENSIVENESS	All essential data is collected for every person served by the agency or organization. All or most of the factors that are considered important for understanding and analyzing events and the issues under review are included in the database. .
UTILITY	Information and data is useful and practical. It is easy to understand and can be readily used for assessment and to make real changes in practice.
CONFIDENTIALITY & ACCESSIBILITY	Information meets all applicable confidentiality and privacy requirements and is available to the people who need to use it. Information and data can be accessed in a variety of formats and using different methods.
TIMELINESS	Information is current and reflects what is happening now, not a long time in the past. It can be used to guide decisions.
PARSIMONY	Information is not duplicative and is as simple as necessary to understand the issue. Data is streamlined to show only the variables that are useful to the targeted task in order to prevent confusion and information overload.
INTEGRATION	Data is easily linked to related information and other data systems. The linkages allow easy analysis of the relationship of the issue under study to other variables that are captured within the organization's information management systems so that a more holistic picture can be generated of performance, quality and risk/safety. When combined with other data, important patterns affecting quality and risk are revealed.
ORGANIZATION & ANALYSIS	Data is arranged and organized in an orderly fashion so that it can be easily read and understood. It is organized to facilitate analysis and is able to be presented in myriad formats (e.g., graphs, charts). The analysis of data meets professional standards and is performed by qualified persons on a regular basis. It identifies issues and trends that can improve the safety and quality of services and supports.
COMMUNICATION	Data summaries and reports are issued on a regular basis to inform and promote the establishment of prevention and improvement initiatives. The format used to report data and the complexity of the information is customized to the audience for which it is intended. Findings are explained and referenced to pertinent benchmarks, and distributed to various levels of the organization, with possible inclusion of public reporting.

GENERAL CONCERNS WITH THE USE OF DATA

IN ADDITION to the more specific issues associated with data quality that were reviewed in the previous section, there are some very basic issues and general concerns related to the use of data as a performance measurement and quality improvement tool. These potential "problems" should be periodically assessed as organizations establish, modify, enhance and expand the data systems that they use on a regular basis.

These general issues are somewhat ubiquitous. They affect almost all major businesses that collect and utilize data, not just those in the field of I/DD. For instance, the Wall Street Journal[1] identified five mistakes common to companies that use and rely on large databases. These "mistakes" can impact service systems and organizations supporting people with disabilities the same way they can affect the performance of large companies that are not in the field of human services. The five mistakes noted by the Wall Street Journal are:

1. Focusing on data without first identifying the aim or goal of analyzing and using the information, or, "data for data's sake."

2. Attempting to analyze data using personnel without the requisite skill sets (e.g., statistical and analytical solutions expertise), or, what the WSJ referred to as a "talent gap."

3. Collecting too much data, causing confusion and wasting money, time and resources that could be used more productively in other endeavors, or, "data, data everywhere."

4. Competition between managers and organizational units over what data to collect and analyze and related to the "ownership" of the information and its use. The WSJ article refers to this mistake as company "infighting."

5. Beginning the use of objective analytics by designing overly complex and expensive data initiatives rather than gradually building capacity and "chunking" data collection, organization and analysis into more manageable phases, or, "aiming too high."

Experience suggests that these very same mistakes are extremely common in many I/DD organizations and large public disability oversight systems. It is therefore strongly recommended that careful consideration be given to the identification and correction of these issues before they can negatively impact on the acceptance of data as a useful tool in risk management efforts. **Appendix C** (Fixing General Problems with Your Data) provides a simple tool for identifying the presence of these issues and developing a plan to correct them.

Special Note: More detailed information regarding specific data system design and analytic approaches can be found in the *Risk Management in DD* series, especially in the on-line courses and books that focus on *Mortality Review and Reporting in DD* and *Incident Management in DD*.

MINIMIZING BIAS

A WIDE VARIETY OF FACTORS can bias[iii] the data that is collected and analyzed and in so doing can negatively influence the validity and reliability of the data itself and the results of any analysis. Most causes of such bias or distortion in the data are usually not intentional. They are simply artifacts of how the data is collected, organized and/or analyzed. It is very important to try to identify and then minimize sources of bias whenever possible to ensure that the results of the data analysis provide the most accurate information possible and do not lead to inaccurate conclusions. Of course, it is not reasonable nor is it realistic to control every single source of bias present in a set of data. Nonetheless, it is important to recognize potential bias when determining how much emphasis to put on different sets of data.

There are many possible causes of data bias. Three of the more important factors that are often present in I/DD data systems and that should be considered when evaluating the quality of an I/DD system are:

1. **SYSTEM CHARACTERISTICS.** The "culture" regarding the importance of recognizing, reporting and correcting problems is usually different across organizations and even within specific programs or sites within any one organization. While senior leaders set the tone and expectations that shape this "cultural bias," program managers and site supervisors also play an important role. Therefore, carefully consider the potential systems bias that may exist whenever reviewing data. Always ask this question: "*Are there any differences in the level of 'motivation' to report data?*" and think about the following types of related issues:

   - *Is data based on self-report or independent review?* Self-reported data may be less reliable and valid since there is a natural tendency to shy away from reporting incidents that reflect poor performance or failure.

   - *Is reporting voluntary or mandatory?* If voluntary, reporting may not be a high priority in certain programs whereas in other settings it receives a high priority.

   - *Are there consequences for non-reporting? Are they applied consistently? What are the chances of being caught?* If it "doesn't matter" whether or not reports are made, there may be less likelihood data is complete and accurate.

   - *If reported, is there a potential for negative consequences to the reporter?* A punitive environment will often suppress reporting since identifying a failure may lead to disciplinary action.

   - *What systems are in place to identify non-reporting or inaccurate reporting?* Very often there are not meaningful checks in place to measure and assure consistent and accurate reporting; this can lead to reporting errors and an insidious breakdown in the actual implementation of reporting requirements.

[iii] Bias is error that stems from how data is collected, analyzed and reported that changes the appearance of the truth.

- *Are there "cultural" differences between organizations/settings with regard to the perceived importance of reporting?* Always consider the strength of the "culture of safety" when assessing the potential for reporting bias.

2. **REPORTER CHARACTERISTICS.** Different people are often responsible for reporting incidents and other related data within and across organizations. The type of personnel, level, training and responsibility of staff and other reporters can play a critical role in determining the accuracy of the data that is reported and then ultimately used to evaluate quality and make decisions about the need for change. It is imperative that those who collect, analyze and use I/DD data think about the potential for reporter bias that may be present. When doing so, ask whether or not there "*are there differences in the probability that data will be accurately reported?*" by considering the following questions:

   - *Who is responsible for collecting data and reporting?* Level of training, other job responsibilities, time constraints typically present that may interfere with data reporting, etc. should all be considered.
   - *Do staff members work alone or with multiple staff present?* This factor is very important for self-reported data such as injury reports, medication errors or other issues that may reflect poorly on the person making the report.
   - *Are there any differences in skill or capacity to accurately report?* Issues such as language differences, education level and reading/writing skills can significantly influence the accuracy of data reports.
   - *Is one type of data "easier" to document and report than another?* Narrative reports can be very difficult for some persons to complete; but, coded forms can be overly complex and difficult to interpret. The type of information that is reported and the format of how it is reported must be considered when thinking about the potential for reporter bias.

3. **DATA ENTRY PERSONNEL CHARACTERISTICS.** Sometimes initial information and data is sent to a second or third party for entry into a database. This is often present when reports are not electronically generated and then automatically flow into a data system. Introducing a third party into the flow of information can help to reduce reporting and recording errors; but, it can also result in additional bias. Therefore, when a reporting system uses separate persons for data entry (especially when there is more than one individual), it is important to assess whether or not there "*are differences in the probability that reports will be accurately documented and consistently entered into a database?*" This can be done by considering the following questions:

   - *Who receives the information? Is it the same person who is responsible for entering the data?* Is it one individual, or can many different persons receive it and enter the data into a database? The more people involved, the greater the likelihood of bias.
   - *Are there differences in how data is communicated and recorded, e.g., by phone, over the internet, filling out a form?* Multiple methods may facilitate timely reporting, but they also tend to introduce substantial issues in reliability of recording the information.

- *Are forms complicated or difficult to read or interpret? Is the language complicated and technical?* Complex reporting forms can lead to incomplete or inaccurate reporting that must then be corrected by the data entry person, leading to the potential for misinterpretation, assumption, speculation and error. What gets entered is not necessarily what actually happened.

- *Is one group more or less likely to record data accurately and quickly? Are there any differences in skill or capacity to accurately record?* The training and experience of personnel, their appreciation for how the information is actually used to generate reports, and the timeliness of data entry to assure reports are up-to-date can all influence the potential for bias.

GENERAL SOLUTIONS FOR PREVENTING BIAS

WHILE IT IS CLEARLY not realistic to completely answer all the questions listed in the previous section, I/DD organizations should attempt to consider as many potential sources of bias as reasonable. Once identified they should then work to address any really BIG issues that might make the data they rely on the most unreliable and/or invalid. Bad data will lead to bad decisions and will eventually negatively impact the quality of services and supports.

If substantial sources of bias are recognized in the collection and recording of data it is especially important to exercise care and note limitations when reporting on the analyses and conclusions that are drawn from the data. In such circumstances it is also important to seek additional evidence from other sources and look for a convergence of information that can validate or support findings and data-based conclusions. Efforts to minimize the source of the bias should always be implemented whenever possible. If this is not done on a regular basis the data will soon become ignored by decision makers within the organization.

A few examples of potential solutions for identified issues that may result in bias include:

- **Modification of reporting formats:** Consider the use of less technical and more conventional terminology on report forms, inclusion of the 'reporters' in the design of reporting tools and accompanying instructions, instructional sheets that incorporate the use of terms in the primary language of staff, use of drop down menus, inclusion of operational definitions for terms and reporting requirements, and conversion to an automatic electronic reporting system that directly records and organizes data.

- **Enhanced training:** It can be extremely helpful to enhance initial and periodic refresher instruction for reporters and recorders of data, use of practice and feedback approaches to training, and incorporating into the program development process the training of service recipients to enhance self-reporting of serious incidents.

- **Changing the organizational culture:** Perhaps most important of all are efforts to establish an organizational culture that promotes reporting as a means of identifying problems so they can be fixed - as opposed to punishing personnel for errors and failures. In a similar fashion organizations should work to communicate and highlight positive changes that have resulted from reporting issues promptly and correctly. They should reward the implementation of solutions that have been generated at the local level and that have been driven by staff identification of actual and potential problems.

> **Tip:** When reviewing data always think about factors that could bias the data. This is especially true for data based on self-report (such as when staff is asked to report on his or her own actions, e.g. abuse/neglect reporting, reporting on medication errors, and many types of incident reports) - as opposed to data based on a review by an independent party. Reports from an independent party usually remove the potential for negative consequences for the reporter.

PROMOTING THE QUALITY OF DATA

THERE ARE A NUMBER of actions that can be taken by most any I/DD organization to better ensure that the data being used can meet expected standards of quality. A few critical considerations for achieving this include:

1. **Carefully define the data set.** An important first step for any analysis is identifying exactly who is going to be included in the dataset that will be used for the analysis. It is absolutely essential to make sure to carefully examine the scope - or comprehensiveness - of the population under consideration. In other words, does it include everyone that is to be represented in the analysis? This critical first step is often overlooked at first and not recognized until the results of a preliminary analysis raise questions. Once you are certain about who (population) is to be included, then proceed to validate the data that is associated with this population (i.e., determine its accuracy and completeness). Remember that incomplete or inaccurate data will yield confusing and inaccurate results. Attention to defining your data set up-front will make the analytic process flow more smoothly and yield results that are more valid and complete.

   a. *Be Comprehensive.* When setting up the data system think broadly and be "comprehensive" when looking at the population to be included in the dataset. Ideally, any surveillance (monitoring) methods or data analysis related to risk management and quality assurance will include <u>all</u> people with which an organization works or for whom they have responsibility. For example, when examining the frequency of a specific type of critical incident that can occur for service recipients it is necessary to include incidents for all persons served. This initial perspective (recognizing the entire population that is served by an organization) will provide an important context for any subsequent use of the data.

   b. *Use Subsets.* Because the role of an organization can often vary for different groups of service recipients, further subgrouping of information may be needed. For example, an organization may provide structured residential services for some individuals that includes primary responsibility for service recipient health, safety and well-being. The same organization may also only provide periodic or selective services (e.g., day program) for other individuals and have a more limited capacity to affect the health and welfare of the person. In other situations, the very same organization may provide very intermittent support and only partial funding for limited at-home services. Because the nature and intensity of support and responsibility varies – and therefore the relative influence the agency has on the topic under analysis, it may be appropriate to break out statistics across service lines. Therefore it is important to carefully analyze such variation when setting up data systems and organizing data for later analyses.

> **Tip:** Break-out population and risk/quality-related data according to service lines when the degree of responsibility for health and safety varies by the type of service and support that an organization provides.

2. **Validate the data.** Once the base population is selected, the next step is to examine whether or not information about all of the people in the selected population is actually included in the data used for the analysis. It is not unusual for data to be incomplete (e.g., not reported or inaccurately documented), especially for cases where the organization does not provide direct and ongoing support or where individuals have been temporarily transferred for service (e.g., temporary nursing home care).

   a. *Beware of incomplete data.* Sometimes information can be incomplete due to the limitations of data collection systems. For example, if an organization only has information on hospitalizations for people who receive residential supports, they would want to pair these incidents with population figures that only include persons receiving residential services instead of the entire service recipient population.

   b. *Compliance may be an issue.* In other cases, data may be incomplete due to a lack of compliance with reporting guidelines or other related factors which prevent information from being included in the data set. For any information collection system, it's important to try to understand the level of procedural compliance. For example, one should explore whether or not all hospital visits are actually being entered into the data system? If not, why not? (One should then question which are likely to be missing and is the missing or incomplete data related to a certain type of service recipient or line of service, etc.? Or are they related to a certain type of hospitalization or even a specific hospital?) In addition it is important to review whether or not certain programs, sites or locations are reporting the same way as other programs, sites or locations. These kinds of variation can significantly affect the accuracy and resultant validity of any analyses. Attention to such issues up-front can save considerable time and effort later on.

> **Tip:** Make sure the data (including population figures) that will be used are complete, consistent across groups, aligned and are not missing service recipients.

METHODS TO VALIDATE DATA

THERE ARE TWO primary methods for performing validation checks of the type of data typically used in I/DD programs. *Internal validation* uses additional information from within the service system to confirm that the information is complete, while *external validation* uses information outside of the service system for this confirmation.

INTERNAL VALIDATION. I/DD service organizations often have multiple pathways for record-keeping and tracking of information. Internal validation is typically a relatively fast and somewhat easy form of validation due to the ready access to multiple sources of information. For example, electronic data systems may link internal records across reporting pathways for each service recipient, which can assist this validation. Electronic data systems may even have automatic validation mechanisms built into them. However, the information used to conduct the internal validation may be subject to the same under- or over-reporting issues as the information being validated. For this reason, internal validation may be a good first step, but may need to be supplemented by the use of external validation procedures.

As an example, in order to validate reports of mortality, many I/DD systems have information on the discharge of people from their service system, including information about the reason for discharge (or transfer). This information can used to identify any unreported deaths that may not be available within the regular death reporting process. For self-reported event data, local information logs can be useful for validating the reporting of events into a system-wide information system where an event report may take more time to complete. The need for implementing internal validation processes should be carefully considered when reviewing results following data collection, especially if and when such results deviate from expectations or appear especially unusual.

> **Tip:** Identify potential sources of information that can be used to perform internal validation of important data within the risk management system. Conduct trials to assess the reliability and validity of selected data sets to help determine where modifications to data collection need to be instituted. Do this on a periodic basis.

EXTERNAL VALIDATION. External information can be useful for validation purposes because it is often less likely to experience the same reporting biases or errors as internal data and may therefore have an even greater ability than internal information to reveal validity issues. However, these external sources of information may unfortunately have unique errors of their own. Because of this, the quality of the external information should be carefully assessed before it is used.

For example, when preparing mortality reports in an I/DD organization, external validation should typically be utilized to confirm whether or not all reportable deaths have been captured. In this instance, a good external source of information about deaths is the Social Security Death Index. The index contains information about deaths reported to the Social Security Administration for people with social security numbers. Of course, one major weakness of this database is that it does not contain information on *all* deaths in the US. Therefore this data source may be more useful for identifying deaths that were not reported in internal systems through cross-checking people recently discharged from the system. It may be less useful for identifying deaths that were falsely reported.

As another example, reporting systems that collect information about medical events may be useful for external validation. Consider hospitalizations – data regarding these events can be validated through information about paid claims that may be available from the review of Medicaid or Medicare data systems.

> **Tip:** Explore and pre-identify potential sources of data that can be used for purposes of external validation and that can be accessed easily. Experiment with cross-checking the data to assess the reliability and validity of your primary data source.

ADDRESSING PROBLEMS IN VALIDITY. When issues are found with the validity of data it can be useful to review the potential for bias in order to try to identify the cause of the potential problem(s). For example, is there confusion about reporting rules? Do different subgroups use the information system differently? Or is there a common reason why information may be missing, such as limited information availability in a certain service line? Once identified, it is possible to target the remediation to the cause. In this regard one should first consider simple interventions including any or all of the following:

- Strengthen operational definitions
- Revise training protocols
- Reduce narrative fields on report forms
- Clarify reporting and recording responsibilities

> **Tip:** Always try to understand why problems with reporting may be taking place. Do not automatically assume failure to adhere to established protocols is due to simple noncompliance by reporters. It can be helpful to carefully review and address common causes of adherence failures by reviewing **Appendix E:** 7 Common Reasons for Staff Error.

Chapter 5
Collecting Data

THE METHODS THAT ARE EMPLOYED and the design of the tools that are used to collect information within an I/DD service organization or large disability system is critical to and forms the foundation for informative data analysis. The structure of the tools that are used is one of the most significant factors for determining the completeness, utility and quality of the data that is collected and ultimately analyzed. The process of data collection will therefore influence the accuracy of findings and conclusions that are drawn from the analysis of the data and the ultimate decisions that result from consideration of those findings.

The collection of information (data) for the analysis will usually involve a number of processes, each of which has various advantages as well as disadvantages. For example, critical incident data may come from electronic reporting systems or, at times, involve paper forms that are submitted, faxed or mailed to a central location for data input or recording within an organization. Other information may come from program logs or even internal electronic billing or registry systems. Well-designed data collection tools for each of these processes is important for assuring consistency and reliability across various reporters and different programs and areas within an organization.

REVERSE ENGINEERING DATA COLLECTION TOOLS

THE DESIGN OF DATA COLLECTION tools should be directly related to what information is needed and that will be analyzed and reported on. In other words, it is essential that one clearly understand what is needed to complete any analysis of data and only then to make sure the information collection process can provide it. Unfortunately, many data reporting and collection processes in I/DD systems have evolved by focusing first on collecting information only to find out later on that the available data is not what is really needed. This type of problem and the resultant inefficiencies it creates can be reduced by "thinking ahead" and using an approach known as reverse engineering.

Such reverse engineering is unfortunately the opposite of how many data systems evolve in the field of I/DD. It is all too common for disability service organizations to focus on developing collection protocols first and then establishing elaborate systems to record and organize the data next, before designing methods for the analysis and reporting of the data. This can lead to wasted time and resources since once reporting has begun policies will have already been developed and staff trained. Only at this point do data analysts (too often) realize that what is really needed by users is not available. This requires the redesign of data collection tools, additional time and expenses for the recoding of data systems, the need to retrain staff and other reporters and the rewriting of existing policies and procedures. Confusion, increased error and frustration can and often are the end products of this lack of foresight. Consequently, it is strongly recommended that, when possible, organizations prepare for data analysis by beginning with an appreciation for what will ultimately be needed and only then design an information collection approach that will generate that information.

In this regard, it can be very helpful to develop a "mock" analytic report that includes samples of tables and graphs that will be needed and that are desired by the users of the data. This can better assure that relevant information will be actually available in the information collection tools, demographic databases and/or other processes for information collection and management that are used by the organization.

> **Tip:** Before spending too much time and significant resources on the design of data management systems and reporting protocols, try to identify what specific information you want to include in reports and what types of analyses you want to conduct with the data. This should drive the design of the data system. **Appendix F** contains a checklist that can be used to help plan the development of data systems and reports (Checklist for Reverse Engineering Data Management Systems).

FORMATTING DATA ENTRY FIELDS

THE FORMAT OF DATA REALLY DOES MATTER! It is extremely important to pay careful attention to how data collection systems are set up. Similar to the reverse engineering concept discussed previously, for data that is manually entered into a database or spreadsheet, it's especially important to plan the format of the data before it begins to be entered. Some information will have a natural format, such as a date or a number. However, for fields that use text or predetermined categories, a more structured format should be established and required for data entry. Consistency in using the prescribed format is critical for assuring proper data analysis. For example, when entering information pertaining to gender, one needs to decide ahead of time whether reporters should enter M or F as opposed to using the respective words "male" or "female." If a mix of both formats is used, "M" and "male" will appear to be different categories and result in inaccuracies and confusion. While this example is simple and straightforward, inconsistencies in data reporting and recording can present more complicated challenges for the data analyst when working with other more complex data fields (such as categories like 'contributing factor' or 'environment'). This issue represents just one more reason for using structured objective data fields as opposed to narrative fields when setting up data collection formats and recording information for use in data analysis

.

Yes/No Fields. For many data fields, a simple "Yes/No" response can be used. However, before establishing this type of field one should carefully consider the following issues:

- Care needs to be taken to assure that "Yes/No" options do not overly constrain the responses, causing them to become less informative or, worse yet, forcing recorders to make choices that aren't relevant or accurate. One example where two response options may not be appropriate is when information may not be known at the time of reporting. In such instances it can be helpful to use a specific entry that specifies the data is not known (e.g., "Unknown"). This can help differentiate the legitimate "unknown" entries from blank fields that may represent a data field that has not yet been completed. For example, if one wanted to analyze how many people used hospice services prior to death, the entry field could ask the question "Were hospice or comfort care measures used?" Here the entry could be restricted to "Yes," "No" or "Unknown."

- For other categories of information there may be situations where a less specific or "in-between" answer is required such as when the concept of "partial" is required. For example, if asking whether a service recipient requires assistance with walking, there can be important distinctions between always needing assistance and only requiring such assistance in certain situations. A simple "Yes/No" response would not be appropriate in this example.

- With some data fields, important information can be lost if restricted to a simple "Yes" or "No" response. For example, when reporting injuries, the severity of the injury is usually an important piece of information needed by a service provider and/or oversight agency. In this instance a simple "Yes/No" response would usually be inadequate (i.e., it is important to differentiate between a minor injury such as a bruise and an injury requiring medical treatment). Often categories such as this need to be followed up with additional data fields that allow more detail to be recorded.

Therefore, with many "Yes/No" categories - as well as other instances when structuring how data is organized is critical it is important to consider how different users of the data may want and need to view the information. Data entry formats should then be structured to include the smallest level of detail that will be necessary to provide such information. In the field of I/DD for example, managers and quality assurance personnel typically want to see data broken out into local program areas. In other instances, clinical staff may need to see greater detail regarding hospital visits than is desired by a non-clinical audience. That is why it is so important to keep the different end users in mind when deciding how to best format data collection systems and organize the data for later analysis.

To accomplish this it is often useful to structure data so that smaller and more detailed information within categories can easily "roll-up" to broader levels which are usually more useful to managers and other personnel that oversee more major units within the organization. The goal in organizing data is to strike a balance between including enough information to make the analysis useful to varied audiences without overly burdening those providing the information; which can quickly lead to disincentives to reporting and/or negative impact on the reliability of the information due to confusion, unreasonable and burdensome time requirements or overly complicated reporting categories.

Narrative vs. Form Fields. While it may be necessary to have one or more narrative fields on an information collection tool, most of the data collection process should be comprised of objective data fields (e.g., check boxes, drop down descriptors) that represent specific questions with pre-determined and structured responses. The use of objective data fields is important to:

- Ensure that consistent and specific information is included in all reports. [When more open-ended questions are asked of the reporter, responses will tend to be quite variable, increasing the probability that critical information will not be provided or will vary from one reporter to another].

- Collect data in a structure that is well organized and useful for later data analysis. [Instead of broad open-ended questions, specific categories can be used to help group responses in a consistent fashion. This will prove extremely useful and promote reliability and efficiency when performing later analysis and reporting results].

> **Tip:** Attempt to limit the use of narrative fields or open-ended questions in information collection tools. Design the tools so they emphasize and include objective data fields as much as possible. Use check boxes and drop down lists that can assure information is consistent across reporters and is structured in a way that is most useful for later analysis. Think ahead to save time and effort and reduce frustration later on.

FREQUENCY OF DATA COLLECTION

THE FREQUENCY WITH which data is collected is dependent upon a number of factors including the type of data and the effort required to collect it - balanced against available resources and how the data is to be used (its aim or purpose). It is important to be realistic and practical when establishing data recording and reporting requirements. Less data that can be counted on (i.e., data that is reliable and valid) is better than massive amounts of data that are inaccurate and inconsistent. Therefore it is strongly recommended that organizations are practical when establishing requirements for data reporting.

One common type of data collected within I/DD systems is based on events, i.e., each time the specific type of event occurs, information is reported. This type of data (e.g., critical incident data) is typically collected on an on-going basis, and usually within a rather short duration after the event. The occurrence of the event prompts the generation of data.

Collection of other types of data may be initiated in other ways. For example, satisfaction data may be collected through a survey that is generated on a regular interval (e.g., an annual satisfaction survey); or it may also be related to an event – such as after the receipt of a particular service (e.g., entrance into a program). This latter type of data is often used by commercial retailers or service providers. I/DD organizations may want to measure similar individual-level or organizational-level performance and/or outcomes. For measurement of long-term outcomes, consideration should always be given to striking a reasonable balance between allowing sufficient time for an intervention (e.g. a new or different service provided to a person, or a systems change) to result in the desired outcome versus short enough time interval for the intervention to have had an effect.

> **Example:** Consider a new employment initiative targeted at young adults in a particular service area. The long-term goal may be for a certain proportion of participants to attain a job. When considering the best frequency for such an outcome it may be unreasonable to measure this job attainment within just a month after the start of the program. A longer interval, such as every quarter, may be a more appropriate tool to measure progress. Much longer time periods, however, such as one or more years could allow too many other variables unrelated to the employment initiative itself to cause or contribute to any changes noted by the data.

Another type of data that I/DD organizations often collect is associated with monitoring activities. This type of data may assess whether activities are completed within prescribed timeframes, or even within established cost standards. Monitoring data can also include process outcomes that signal whether or not activities necessary to meet long-term outcomes are being completed as required. Monitoring data is especially relevant to the area of risk and safety management.

> **Example:** In the employment initiative discussed in the previous example, before a job is attained, there are a variety of short-term outcomes that can signal meaningful progress toward the ultimate goal (getting a job) of the initiative. Related data could include measurement of process outcomes. An example of such would be the number of interviews completed, or the number of new employer connections made by the program. While these activities may not always result in the desired outcome, they would be considered important steps that demonstrate desired actions toward attaining the ultimate goal. The frequency of this type of process data can be pre-established, e.g., monthly reporting.

DATA COLLECTION & ITS ANALYSIS

The frequency with which data can and commonly is analyzed will also vary, often in ways very similar to the requirements for the collection of the data itself. In this regard, when considering the analysis of data, it can be helpful to conceptualize the process of analysis as falling into one of three categories:

- Simple aggregate analysis
- More in-depth aggregate analysis, and
- Event or failure analysis that focuses on a single event or process and which is typically used to answer "why" questions

The table on the next page describes the typical level of resource, complexity and the usual frequency for these three categories of analysis.

Characteristics of Three Types of Data Analysis

Type of Analysis	What it is	Resource Requirement	Complexity	Frequency
SIMPLE AGGREGATE ANALYSIS	Aggregation of a small amount of recent data – useful for monitoring activities	Usually a low effort is needed to produce the data	Lowest level of complexity – information is meant to be descriptive. Data reports should be simple enough to skim or read quickly "at a glance"	Data is collected, analyzed and used frequently to monitor activities and systems
IN DEPTH ANALYSIS	More in-depth analysis than needed for simple aggregate reports - often uses information that represents longer duration of time	Requires more resources to produce than simple aggregate reports	Can identify more complex patterns and help inform whether small short-term changes are reflective of trends or just normal fluctuations	Used less frequently than simple aggregate reports, such as for preparing annual reports
EVENT OR PROCESS ANALYSIS	A comprehensive analysis of an event or limited pattern of events that have already occurred or of a process or activity that is planned using information from various sources. Examples include Root Cause Analysis, Failure Mode and Effects Analysis, Factor Analysis, etc.	Reserved for more highly valuable processes - requires a significant amount of effort	May be complex. The goal is to understand systemic factors that are responsible for an event in order to prevent similar events from happening in the future	Should be used strategically on sentinel events or proactively on selected processes where systemic failures could lead to particularly adverse events so that failures are identified before those events can occur

GATHERING DATA WITH LIMITED RESOURCES: USING ESTIMATION AND SAMPLING

IN MANY INSTANCES it is either not practical or there are insufficient resources to gather information about every single person or event within a large organization or disability service system. That is where the use of statistical estimation and sampling can be extremely useful. For instance, consider an agency that is charged with planning a smoking cessation program across an entire state in the U.S. In order to allocate sufficient resources, the agency first requires an estimate of the proportion of the population that smokes on a regular basis. It's simply not feasible, nor is it necessary, for the agency to count every single person who smokes in the state. For the purpose of the resource allocation planning an estimate will suffice. A practical approach for generating this type of estimate would be to count the number of people that smoke in a smaller group of state residents that is representative of the state's overall population. This smaller group is called a *sample*. From the information about smoking in the sample, the agency can then reasonably estimate the prevalence of smoking across the entire state. While the use of a sample may not provide the exact statewide rate of smoking, it will provide a representative range within which the statewide rate likely falls.

Illustration of a Sample Drawn from a Population

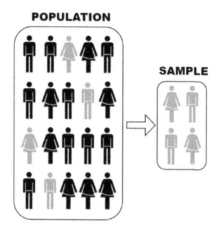

Sampling has a number of advantages in situations where new information needs to be gathered and estimates are considered an adequate method for measurement. A few examples include:

- A satisfaction survey is sent via mail. It may be cost prohibitive to send a survey to every person within a large organization or service system, but a sample of data may be able to provide useful information for developing targets for quality improvement.

- A paper-based record review needs to be conducted. For example, consider a situation where an agency wants to examine the quality of a planning protocol to be used by staff within the organization's residential services unit. The protocols are stored with the service recipient's paper file at their residence. In this instance it may not be necessary to look at every service recipient's protocol to determine the level of policy adherence and the quality of the information in the protocols used across the agency. Rather, viewing a representative sample may provide sufficient information, with no real advantage stemming from the laborious task of looking at all records.

However, in some cases it may not be appropriate to use a sample. Consider the following circumstances where sampling would not be appropriate. For instance, where:

- An estimate is not sufficient due to legal and/or policy requirements. This may include situations where there is a mandate to collect information on all people, or for all events of a certain type (e.g., death reporting, abuse/neglect allegations).

- The group being examined is very small and complete data collection is practical and easy.

- Information is already collected, and using a sample would not increase efficiency. This situation would apply to an electronic system that is already collecting information on all people or on all incidents. For example, when analyzing patterns in hospital visits collected in an electronic reporting system, it is preferable to include all the relevant incidents in the analysis.

SPECIAL CONSIDERATIONS WHEN SAMPLING

THE METHOD USED to select a sample is very important. Samples that are too small can result in inaccurate estimates. Similarly, samples that are biased or skewed (not representative) can result in estimates that can be very misleading. Therefore a sample must be chosen in a careful and strategic manner. When determining how to best select a sample it is quite important to take into consideration the following factors:

1. **Size.** Always ask: *How big is the sample in relationship to the population under study?* If too few people are included in the sample, the sample may not be a valid representation of the larger population. The number of people required for accurate sampling is based both on the size of the population and the type of estimate desired. Methods for calculating scientifically adequate sample size should be used. For example, consider a population that is comprised of 3,000 people. If sample calculations indicate that the sample size needs to be about 350 people and information is only collected on 100 (i.e., the sample is too small), there will not be sufficient information to formulate a valid estimate within the desired margin of error. [Note: formulas and tools exist to help determine appropriate sample sizes. A summary of this information will be included in future sections of the book. This is one instance where the guidance of a statistician is strongly advised.]

2. **Selection Criteria (Inclusion and Exclusion).** Before finalizing a sample, carefully review how the sample was or will be chosen. If the sample was chosen randomly (i.e., without any preconceived reason for selection) it is more likely to be free of bias and therefore representative of the larger population. If, however, data was collected because of a special concern or only within a group that has data readily available, the sample will probably not be representative. For example, if a provider licensure unit within an I/DD state agency decides to only review providers who are experiencing problems (deficiencies), it would be inappropriate to generalize the findings to all service providers (those with and without problems) licensed by the state agency. [Note: when planning to minimize bias, consider what the sample is being used for, in other words, what the data is trying to estimate. Review what types of factors are suspected to result in different responses. Configure the sample such that it balances these potential biasing variables (i.e., get both or all sides of identified factors

included in the sample). If a sample is selected within a particular sub-group, such as only service providers experiencing problems, make sure that any findings or conclusions are only generalized to the same group that was sampled; for example, only for providers determined to be experiencing problems.]

3. **Differences from Population.** When selecting a sample it is important to ask: *Are there any unique characteristics of the sample that make it different from the larger population?* Characteristics of the sample that should be carefully reviewed include factors such as age, level and type of disability, presence of a behavioral health disorder, type of service or support, type of residence and geographic location. The sample should be as close to the larger population from which it is drawn as possible. If there are major differences in important variables it is not appropriate to generalize any findings to the larger population. When and if this occurs findings from the analysis of the sample can only be applied to the population of persons who have the same characteristics as the sample. This potential source of bias is extremely important in the I/DD field since there are often major differences in the type and intensity of services that are provided and the disability characteristics of service recipients within and across any given service system. Therefore, caution should always be exercised when conclusions are made from sampled data. [Note: Pay attention to the general demographics of the population when selecting a sample. Make sure the sample has similar demographics as the group for which one is seeking an estimate. In some instances it may be better to conduct a very purposeful selection within the sample, referred to as stratification, to assure that characteristics of the sample better match those of the population. Again, the advice of a statistician can be very helpful to assist with the design of a sampling methodology.]

> **Tip:** When reviewing the data for an analysis or from a prepared report, it is very important to keep in mind what specific population the information can reasonably apply to Do NOT over generalize the population (i.e., apply the findings to types of groups that weren't included in the sample). The analysis is relevant only for the population with similar characteristics as the same sample.

SAMPLING METHODS

There are a number of different ways to select a sample. The most straightforward is simple random sampling. In this method, within any given population of service recipients each person would have an equal chance of being selected for inclusion in the sample, i.e., they could be chosen at random. The advantage of this method is that it is usually representative of the entire population of service recipients. Therefore, it allows conclusions to be drawn from the data analysis that are applicable to the larger service population.

UNDERSTANDING SAMPLE SIZES. As reviewed previously, the number of people that are required for a sound sample is based both on the size of the population and the type of estimate desired. Determining the size of a sample is therefore based on the amount of information needed to create a useful estimate of the true value of a variable in the larger population. A *useful* estimate is one that we can be relatively certain accurately represents the population; this "certainty" is referred to as a confidence level. It also requires that the sample is precise enough to be used, called a margin of error. For example, an estimate of between 60-70% is more useful than an estimate of between 40-90%. These two factors – confidence level and precision (or margin of error) are used in determining how much information (the size of our sample) is needed.

The more information that is collected in the sample, the smaller the margin of error will be; leading to greater confidence that the measurement of the population actually falls within the estimated range. This means that the estimate will be closer to the true value of the population.

Example: *Assume an organization distributes a survey to its service recipients to assess their satisfaction with the services that have been provided by their case managers. The table below describes how these concepts would apply to the hypothetical sample.*

Description of Concept	How It Applies to the Example
Point Estimate: When a sample is selected, the information from this sample is used to generate a **point estimate** of a measurement for the larger population.	In the sample of consumers, 80% were satisfied with their case manager. Therefore, the point estimate for the population is 80%.
Precision/Margin of Error: The point estimate may not be the exact measurement of the population, but with proper methods it should be relatively close. In order to understand how close, one would use a **margin of error**. If the sample is unbiased, the true measurement of the population likely falls within this margin of error, often written as +/-. The smaller the margin of error that is desired, the larger the sample size that will be required.	If a sample size was used that was calculated to collect enough information for a margin of error of 5%, then 80% +/- 5% (equal to 75% to 85%) of the population is likely satisfied with their case manager.
Confidence Level: The confidence level describes the chance that the true value for the population falls outside of the range generated by the margin of error associated with the point estimate. The higher the value, the more confidence there is in the estimate. Typically, values of 90% or 95% are used to generate estimates for most I/DD service systems. (Remember: When selecting a confidence level it is advisable to consult a statistician If this resource is not available, it is recommended that a 95% value is used).	If enough information was collected for a 95% confidence level then the organization can be 95% sure that 75% to 85% of the service recipient population was most likely satisfied with their case manager. In other words, there is only a 5% chance that this estimate is wrong. This represents a relatively small chance that the true satisfaction level is outside of the 75% to 85% range; resulting in a high level of confidence for the obtained estimate.

CALCULATING SAMPLE SIZES

SAMPLE SIZE FORMULAS will differ depending on what it is that that needs to be estimated. For example, different formulas would be used for estimating (1) a proportion – often useful when discussing measures with categories, and (2) an average value – useful when using a continuous measure such as weight.

ESTIMATING A PROPORTION. The following formula can be used for estimating the *proportion* of a population. Using the example from the previous section, this would apply to estimating what proportion of the population is satisfied with their services from their case manager. To calculate this the formula requires the following information:

- The total size of the population
- An estimate of the proportion that are satisfied. If unknown, use 0.5
- The desired precision
- The desired confidence interval (typically 95%)

$$\text{Sample Size} = \frac{\text{Population Size X (Confidence Level)}^2 \text{ X Proportion "Yes" X Proportion "No"}}{\text{Precision}^2 \text{ X (Population Size - 1)} + \text{(Confidence Level)}^2 \text{ X Proportion "Yes" X Proportion "No"}}$$

For example, if the estimate is being calculated for the first time (no prior experience with this survey), and we assume the following values:

- Population Size = **3,000** (this value can be estimated)
- Proportion satisfied ("Yes") = **.05** or 50% (this a rough estimate since there is no prior experience – if survey used before, can substitute actual proportion that was satisfied)
- Proportion not satisfied ("No") = **.05** (equal to 1 – proportion satisfied)
- Desired precision = **.05** (to get a precision level of +/-5%)
- Confidence level = **1.96** (alpha level for a 95% confidence level that can be copied from a statistical table)

$$\text{Sample Size} = \frac{3000 \text{ X } (1.96)^2 \text{ X .05 X .05}}{(0.5)^2 \text{ X } (3000-1) + (1.96)^2 \text{ X .05 X .05}}$$

Sample Size = 340.65 (round up to 341)

This result means that for a population of about 3,000 service recipients the sample size (number of people that would need to be surveyed) should be at least 341 people in order to attain a precision level of +/- 5% with a 95% confidence level.

NOTE: The on-line course entitled *Data Analysis for Quality improvement* that is available in the *Risk Management in DD* series includes a number of video demonstrations on how to apply this and other statistical formulas presented throughout this book. For more information on accessing the on-line course, interested readers are encouraged to go to: http://www.udiscovering.org/products/risk-management-developmental-disabilities.

ESTIMATING A MEAN. A different formula is used for estimating the average value (e.g., the mean) in a population. An example would be if a service organization wanted to conduct a health initiative and first wanted to estimate the average body mass index of the entire population. Since it would be rather time consuming to calculate this value for every single person, an estimate would probably suffice before starting the health intervention. To generate such an estimate very similar information to the earlier sample size formula would be needed, except the estimated proportion of "yes" and "no" values would be replaced by an estimate of the variance.

The formula for estimating the sample in this instance would require the following information:

- The total size of the population
- An estimate of the variance of the measure in the population.
- The desired precision
- The desired confidence interval (typically 95%)

$$\text{Sample Size} = \frac{\text{Population Size} \times (\text{Confidence Level})^2 \times \text{Variance}}{\text{Precision}^2 \times (\text{Population Size} - 1) + (\text{Confidence Level})^2 \times \text{Variance}}$$

ESTIMATING SIZE FOR A STRATIFIED SAMPLE

IN MANY I/DD SERVICE systems, there are groups of people that can be expected to have rather large differences in the variable that is being measured. For example there would likely be substantial differences in the type and level of support needed by and provided to individuals in different service lines within an organization or large system (e.g., family support v residential v day/vocational services). Instead of leaving the representation of each service line up to chance (as would take place in random selection) a stratified sample could be used to ensure that each service line had equal or proportionate representation in the sample. Collecting a stratified sample can better ensure that an adequate amount of information is collected about each service line, to therefore allowing analytic findings to be generalized to the larger service recipient population.

To perform stratified sampling, the population is first divided into the relevant groups (strata) that will be sampled. It is also possible to sample within these different groups in order to make sure the sample has representatives from each group. This strategy allows one to draw a conclusion about each group separately. In order to perform stratified sampling, there must be sufficient information known about the population or larger group available before sampling is done in order to divide the population into these strata. Random selection is then performed within each group.

When performing stratified sampling, there are two basic methods for dividing the sample across the strata. They are referred to as proportionate sampling and disproportionate sampling.

PROPORTIONATE SAMPLING. In this method, the total sample size is selected based on the proportion of the population represented by the strata or sample group.

Example: Consider an organization with 4 administrative regions. Region 1 has 40% of the population that is served. Regions 2, 3 and 4 each have 20%. To collect a sample of 100 people, one would randomly select 40 people from Region 1 and 20 people from each of Regions 2, 3, and 4. This would ensure that the sample was proportionally the same as the larger service population.

DISPROPORTIONATE SAMPLING. In the second method the sample that is split across the strata is not the same as the proportion of the population it represents. This approach may be useful when there are small strata, as a proportionate sample may not collect enough information to allow meaningful generalization about the subset.

Caution: If a disproportionate sample is used, special methods such as weighting of the strata must be employed in order to correctly analyze the data. It is therefore strongly recommended that a qualified statistician be consulted whenever an I/DD organization uses disproportionate sampling as an estimation technique.

Chapter 6
Preparing for Analysis

IN ORDER TO APPROACH the task of data analysis in a thoughtful and systematic fashion – and avoid having to "backtrack" once the analysis has started - it is first necessary to carefully think about the questions that need to be addressed in the analysis and identify solutions to problems that are likely to arise during the process of data analysis. Time spent on such pre-planning will make the analysis go much smoother later on and help avoid repeated frustrations and wasted effort. To accomplish this, it can be extremely helpful to create an *analysis plan*. Such a plan can include, for instance:

- Critical questions the analysis must answer,

- Considerations about the quality of the data (reliability/validity/completeness),

- The amount of resources and effort that may be required to gather and "clean" the data that will be used in the analysis, and

- The relative priority of the questions to be answered by the analysis (i.e., what are the most important questions and issues that need to be addressed versus what might be "nice" to know, but is not really essential).

It is not unusual to experience limitations on the available resource (e.g., staff, funding) and time (e.g., deadlines) that can be devoted to any specific data analysis. Sharing the analysis plan with management and those who will be using the data can establish realistic expectations and better assure communication and resource commitment across the organization. It will also help to clarify the importance of generating objective answers to the question at hand and make clear urgent requirements for answers to questions that may be emerging (particularly those issues related to safety and serious adverse events). **Appendix G** contains the outline for developing an analysis plan (Summary Data Analysis Plan). It can also be helpful to review **Appendix F** (Checklist for Reverse Engineering Data Management Systems) to help guide in the design of an approach to planned data analysis.

Also remember that when reporting results it is important to note the limitations of the data that was analyzed so that end users can align their expectations with the realities that are present and do not over-interpret findings (a not uncommon bias present in I/DD programs). Taking the time up front to evaluate, set expectations and plan the analysis will prevent frustration and disappointment later on.

Tip: Before beginning a detailed analysis, develop a brief *Data Analysis Plan* to clarify the question(s) that will be the focus of the analysis, assess issues of validity and reliability of the data that will be utilized, anticipate resources that will be required to complete the analysis and note limitations of the findings to help set realistic expectations across the entire organization.

CREATING AN ANALYSIS PLAN

THE DEVELOPMENT of an analysis plan (see **Appendix G**) should always begin with a series of questions. When planning for the analyses of information within most any I/DD service organization or system, start by identifying and articulating the specific question(s) that require answers using data. Understanding what is needed is a necessary condition and essential prerequisite for determining the type of analysis that should be performed.

All too often organizations initiate data analysis while still unsure of exactly what it is they need and want to know. The organization typically has a lot of data and leadership says "*Analyze it!*" As a consequence, personnel focus time and energy on an overly general review of the data that they're aware of or spend time and resource "looking" at different types of data (such as a particular category of reported incidents). This can sometimes not only waste time, but also distract attention away from what is really important and make it more difficult to structure a meaningful analysis later on. The absence of a plan results in wasted efforts that fail to satisfy anyone. *"Looking at data"* will invariably mean different things to different people. Priorities may differ depending on the perspectives and needs of each individual within the organization. For example,

- Leadership may be interested in how the rate of incidents within the organization compares across subgroups (e.g., regions or administrative areas) or how their organization compares to other organizations on a state or national basis.

- Supervisory and clinical staff with a more local focus may be more interested in identifying the leading causes of hospitalization for the population they serve.

> **Remember:** Understand what you need and want to know before starting an analysis. Always try to articulate and seek consensus regarding the specific questions the data analysis must answer. Different people within the organization usually need to review data (i.e., *look at the data*) and the results from good analysis in order to understand what is happening in their programs and areas of responsibility. This almost always means something entirely different to them compared to the staff that will be performing the actual data analysis. Seek clarity before starting.

The process of articulating specific questions such as "What is the rate of hospital visits in each region?" or "Do any programs have more hospital visits than we would expect?" is extremely important. Specific and focused questions will:

- Allow clarity and greater specificity in framing the analysis so the purpose and the constraints of the analysis can be more accurately defined

- Lead to the establishment of a more useful and efficient analysis and save a great deal of time and effort by the data analyst

- Foster common expectations within the organization about what the analysis can and cannot provide

- Align available information with the desired result and aim of the analysis in order to better:

- Identify whether or not the necessary information and data is available to address the target question;

- Help focus attention on whether or not the available data and information is sufficiently valid and reliable in order to accurately answer the question; and,

- Inform questions regarding the cost (time/effort) vs. the benefit (utility) of the analysis that is being planned.

QUESTIONS DATA ANALYSIS CAN HELP ANSWER

WHEN USING DATA to assess the safety and quality of services and supports in an I/DD organization and to help develop improvement goals carefully consider the different types of questions that can be realistically addressed. A few examples are presented below to illustrate important questions that can usually be addressed by data about the safety and quality of supports within a service system:

1. *Where do we stand now?* This type of question helps keep track of specific issues within a service system and can help measure progress toward meeting established goals. Often, data related to this type of question populates monitoring tools such as dashboards and management reports. This type of data is useful for establishing a baseline prior to implementing changes and to use as a means of informing goal-setting efforts. The data related to questions such as this can be useful for initiating discussions with managers and other staff about qualitative and more subtle factors that are taking place in the field and that may contribute to safety and quality issues underlying observed trends and patterns.

There are two primary categories of measurement data that are typically used to answer this type of question:

   a. *Process measures* are typically used for monitoring purposes as a way to inform an organization whether or not its services and support systems are functioning as intended. The data can be used to monitor access to services, the actual delivery of services, adherence to reporting timelines, progress in training or certifications, and a variety of other factors that can be used to identify weakness or concerns of poor quality in the service delivery system. Process-related information can also help to inform whether the foundational services and monitoring systems that are considered necessary for quality outcomes are in place and operating as intended.

   b. *Outcome measures* go beyond process measures and assess the impact of services and support systems. They can include measures about access to health care, achievement of personal goals as identified in service plans, service recipient exercise of choices and freedoms, and events such as critical incidents. They can also include measures of consumer satisfaction, and service recipient assertions about personal experience of quality (e.g. *I feel staff members respect me.*). Meaningful outcome measures can often be challenging to define and measure; however when paired with appropriate process measures they can greatly enhance an organization's understanding about whether or not the processes that are in place are producing the desired outcomes for the people that are served.

2. *How are we doing relative to others like us – and - how are we doing relative to those we consider to be the best?* Answers to this category of questions can help provide added meaning when looking at the performance and status of a service organization by providing comparative benchmarks. Identifying *relative* strengths and weaknesses can provide confirmation of good performance, evidence of less than adequate quality and even supply an objective basis for identifying potential issues affecting the safety and risk of harm for service recipients. While such comparisons can be very useful, they must be made carefully and with caution to prevent erroneous conclusions to be drawn from the data. This is particularly important in the field of I/DD since there are very few standards established for the collection and analysis of data. [More detail regarding this issue is presented in later chapters].

3. *Within our organization/system, where do differences exist?* While system-wide perspectives have value, it can also be important to also look at variations that may exist within the larger system. The *average* pattern expressed by data may not reflect what is happening in discrete units, programs or areas. For example across any given service system, data may show that the rate of medication administration errors has fallen when compared to the previous year. However, if a local program experienced an increase in the rate of errors, this change might not be evident in the overall system's average rate (unless it was an extremely large change). Examining variation across and between service lines, programs, geographic/administrative areas or other groupings can help identify important issues that require further review and possible changes to processes and resource allocations.

4. *Are we changing over time, and if so, how?* Historic data, such as that typically used for answering the first question, *'where do we stand?'* can be used again, when reviewed for multiple time periods to assess change over time. Such information can also be compared to established goals or quality improvement targets. Change data can be extremely important in risk and quality assessment activities. Changes over time, especially if unexpected, may reflect a change in the underlying risk that is present within a specific service or program, or in the quality of your system, triggering the need for further review. Measuring change over time can also help assess the effects of quality improvement initiatives or other service modifications that have been implemented. The use of this type of data can serve to clarify the rate and consistency of change across an organization or large system. It can and should be used to supplement the more common use of subjective anecdote and personal reports of change that are so often the primary basis for evaluation in I/DD services.

5. *Who is at immediate risk?* Program and service coordinator staff can often benefit from using data systems to regularly identify people that fit certain patterns of risk. Using data systems in this manner can provide a useful safety-net to better ensure that important issues and risk factors impacting people's lives are "flagged" and recognized in a timely fashion. This prompts the modification of services and supports more quickly in order to protect the health and welfare of service recipients. Data systems can be configured and used to "kick-out" pre-established patterns of variables and changes in trends over time to trigger selective

reviews and initiate preventive actions. [More detail on generating this type of data report is presented in a later chapter, *Using Results*.]

6. *Why did this pattern occur - and how can we change it in the future?* The question of "why?" something has taken place is typically one of the most important questions that can be asked when managing risk in an I/DD organization. It is also one of the most challenging to meaningfully and directly answer using data. A number of strategies do exist however that can help piece together clues to inform the answer as to why certain patterns and relationships between variables may occur. Approaches such as risk adjustment, examination of the association between factors, sample stratification, the use of risk ratios and the application of certain statistical tests can help provide a basis for identifying "why" certain patterns and relationships are present. [See the next chapter, *Analyzing Your Data* for more detail on using data for this purpose.]

ASSESSING DATA

IT IS EXTREMELY IMPORTANT to evaluate the data that will be used in an analysis before beginning to analyze it. The following example illustrates how to use guided questions to strengthen the planning process prior to starting the actual analysis.

Example: Assume a data analyst in an I/DD service organization receives a request to conduct an analysis designed to answer the question: *"What medical conditions are most responsible for causing people to go to hospital emergency rooms in our agency?"*

Step 1: The analyst needs to ask *"What is the source of the information will we use?"* In doing so, he/she should think carefully about whether or not there is the right information available within the existing data systems to adequately answer this question. For example, does the agency collect information about emergency room visits using an incident reporting form, and if so does it have a report data field that asks the reason for the hospital visit? If not, consider where to obtain the information.

Step 2: Next the analyst must ask *"What is the quality of the data that is available and how might that quality affect the results of the analysis?"* If information about emergency hospital visits and the reason for the visit is not immediately available and must be obtained from another source, the analyst will need to consider how reliable and valid the data is that can be used for addressing the question at hand. In the example regarding ER visits, it will be important to consider who completes the report that does contain the needed information. For instance, are incident reports completed by non-clinical staff? If so, what source of information do these staff members use to complete these fields in the report (e.g., notes from a nurse, their own "non-professional" opinion, etc.)? Differences such as these will affect the level of detail and the clinical relevancy of the data that is entered into the report field, and, will therefore affect the accuracy of the data and its ability to correctly answer the focus question. Other factors to consider are timing of the report (i.e., when the report is completed and the data entered into the database). If, for example, the form is completed immediately after the hospital visit, there may only be very limited and preliminary information available – such as the symptoms that led to the visit. If there is not a mechanism in place to update the report with additional information after discharge, the data that is used in an analysis for answering the question about causes for hospital emergency visits can be of limited value (e.g., if someone goes the emergency room for chest pain, it may not be known if it was due to simple indigestion or a heart attack).

Step 3: Also ask *"Is the data properly structured for this analysis?"* Consider whether or not the data that is available is actually useful in its current form and look carefully at how it is structured. For example, review whether or not it is from an open entry field (i.e., such as when reporters type in responses) or is the data collected via a dropdown menu of pre-defined categories? Open entry fields are more likely to have substantial variability depending on the reporter and often require interpretation or even modification by the analyst. Additionally, such fields often require more time and effort to code in a manner that will be amenable for aggregate analysis. On the other hand, categorical responses can constrain the level of detail available.

Tip: Evaluate the data that you will be using for the analysis. Ask whether or not the data is valid, reliable and structured in such a way that it can be used to answer the most important focus question(s). Special issues may be present for data that is derived from "open" narrative fields when different reporters, with varying skills and training are responsible for data entry. Understand and share these limitations with users and management before proceeding.

REVIEW OTHER POTENTIAL SOURCES OF DATA

WHEN THE SPECIFIC DATA that is needed for an analysis is not directly available, explore other potential sources of information that may be able to provide the needed information. For instance, in the example of emergency room visits presented in the previous section, consider a situation in which there wasn't a specific field on an organization's incident report that captured the reason for emergency room visits? The analyst could look for other sources of information that could capture similar and relevant information such as might be contained in another data field on the incident report or even in a person's medical/health or case file? One could also peruse other fields on the incident report itself. For instance, there could be related information contained within a narrative field, such as a description of the incident that could begin to provide the needed information. In other words, the analyst may need to investigate a variety of documents and alternative sources of data in order to accurately answer questions and complete an analysis. Remember, extracting certain information required for any given data analysis may require a substantial amount of time and effort. That is why the development of an analysis plan ahead of time is so important.

Nonetheless, the need to better understand particular issues such as *"What medical conditions are causing people to go to Hospital Emergency Rooms?"* may be extremely important to an organization and its efforts to improve service quality and better manage health-related risk. When this occurs and there is no readily available data to answer the question, the analyst can consider examining a subset or sample of data that can be accessed. This can allow one to obtain some information that can help answer important question without requiring an extensive commitment of time and resources. Such review may also provide valuable information and guidance on how to improve future data collection so that it can more easily address the kinds of questions that are most important to an organization.

ORGANIZE DATA USING ELECTRONIC FORMATS

In preparation for analyses, always make sure the data is organized, preferably in an electronic format by using a spreadsheet or a simple database. If the organization already uses an electronic data system to collect and store the data that will be used in an analysis, it is likely that the information can be readily exported into a spreadsheet or database. However, when the organization uses an older paper-based system the analyst will most likely need to design and then import the data into a spreadsheet or database. This can require substantial time and effort; but it is usually well worth it in the long term. Once again, the use of an analysis plan ahead of time can identify this type of issue.

Once data has been organized in a spreadsheet or database, the next step is to summarize the data. Summarizing data can help to better recognize possible patterns and may even provide information that can directly address some of the basic questions that have been identified as needing answers through data analysis. Data tables are usually a helpful starting point for summarizing data. This is especially true for data that can be organized by categories. In addition, once the data is structured and summarized it should also be checked for internal consistency.

> **Note:** The on-line course in the *Risk Management* series entitled *Using Data as a Quality Tool in DD* contains more detailed information regarding issues associated with the design and use of an electronic spreadsheet/database for organizing a risk management and quality data system. The on-line course also includes video based step-by-step examples on how to organize and summarize sample I/DD data in a spreadsheet and develop data tables and perform checks for internal consistency. Interested readers are encouraged to explore the additional resources contained in the on-line course. To access the on-line course go to: http://www.udiscovering.org.

Chapter 7
Analyzing Data

SIMPLE METHODS TO SUMMARIZE DATA USING DESCRIPTIVE STATISTICS

BEYOND BASIC TABLES there are some other simple ways in which common I/DD data can be easily summarized and understood by most personnel. Descriptive statistics represents one such method and includes a variety of relatively simple approaches to examining basic aspects of data, including the:

- Midpoint
- Dispersion
- Frequency

Summarizing data in this fashion is extremely useful before proceeding with more complex analyses or even beginning to compare one data set with another. Two very common categories of descriptive statistics that are especially useful when reviewing typical I/DD system data include, measures of *central tendency* and *measures of dispersion*.

MEASURES OF CENTRAL TENDENCY

A VERY BASIC and useful way to summarize data is to calculate one or more measures of central tendency. These statistics describe features about the "middle range" of your data. Understanding where the middle of the data falls, and then how the data falls around this midpoint can identify important differences between data from year-to-year or in comparison to other populations. Three important measures of central tendency are the mean, median and mode.

MEAN. The mean is often called the *average* and is the midpoint of the range of a group of numbers. It is calculated by adding the numbers in the data set together and then dividing this sum by the count of the numbers. For example, if we have 5 people aged 25, 34, 46, 50 and 55, the mean is $(25+34+46+50+55)/5 = 42$.

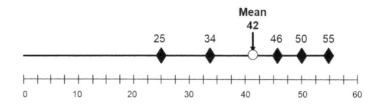

The mean can be useful for describing the center of a range of numbers. It is helpful in understanding what is happening "in general" or "on average." However, the mean is extremely limited since it does not provide information about where the other numbers in the data set fall in relation to the middle or midpoint of the distribution. For example, the numbers may fall evenly on each side of the center. Or, there may be a cluster of numbers on one side, and only few observations that are more extreme on the other. The mean is easily distorted by extreme values and can be subject to rather wild swings if the sample size is small and there are one or more outliers (extreme scores). It should therefore be used with caution and any major "unevenness" in the distribution should be noted when reporting the data. An over reliance on the use of the mean can mask trends or patterns in the data that may be very important. Therefore, when reviewing I/DD system data that uses the mean, especially when comparing different programs or variables over time, one should also include measures of dispersion such as the range (low to high) or amount of deviation in the numbers to make there is a more complete and accurate presentation of findings from the data analysis.

> **Special Consideration:** Reporters and users of data should always beware of extreme numbers or outliers when incorporating the mean as the measure of central tendency. Although it is often used, it can be highly influenced by numbers that are not "typical" for the population, especially when that population is relatively small as often takes place when analyzing data in many I/DD organizations.

As an example of how using the mean alone can be quite misleading, examine the two graphs below. The first presents the average number of physical restraints recorded for two different programs (Programs A and B) over a four year time period (Fiscal Years). The first graph suggests that both programs were similar in the use of restraint since the data only presents the average use over the four years.

Graph 1
Average No. Restraints
FY 2000-2003

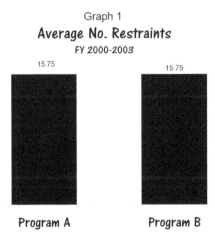

15.75   15.75

Program A   Program B

57

However, a completely different picture emerges when the same data is presented as the yearly number of recorded restraints for each program by year. As can be seen in the second graph (illustrated below), one program (A) witnessed a slight but steady decline while the other (B) experienced a rather dramatic increase in restraint use over time. The use of just the four year average is quite misleading and hides important differences between the two programs. In order to better identify potentially important patterns such as illustrated in this example, it can be helpful to use multiple types of descriptive statistics and summaries to describe the data.

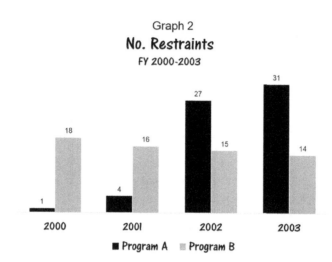

Graph 2
No. Restraints
FY 2000-2003

■ Program A   ▨ Program B

MEDIAN. The median is another very common measure of central tendency. It is the middle number in a distribution of numbers. If a group of numbers is sorted in order (e.g., high to low), the median is the observation (number) in the middle of the distribution of numbers. If there is an even number of numbers, the median equals the midpoint between the two numbers in the middle. The median can be very useful when describing certain variables since it is less affected by extreme values than the mean is. For instance, if we use the same five people in the age example cited above, the median would be 46. Note that in this example the mean is lower than the median because there are two ages - 25 and 34 - that are farther away from each other on the lower end of the range. The other three ages, 46, 50 and 55, are closer together on the higher end of the range. The more extreme low age of 25 leads to a decrease in the value of the mean. Thus the mean is smaller than the median.

Comparing the mean and the median values can provide insight as to whether or not the distribution of the data may be *skewed* (i.e., the data is not distributed equally around the midpoint). If the mean and median are approximately equal, this may indicate little skew to the data (i.e. the data is spread out equally from the mean on both sides). However, if there is greater variation between the median and mean values in a distribution, the data is likely skewed away from the median. In the example cited above and illustrated on the next page, the data is skewed toward the left (i.e., there are fewer observations to the left) and the median is to the right of the mean. In general, the median is often a better way to describe the central tendency data that is skewed.

58

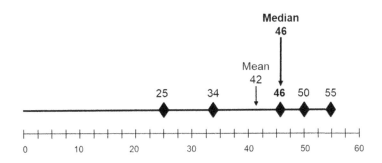

MODE. The mode is the most frequent value within a group of numbers. When analyzing data from I/DD systems, the mode tends to be most useful for non-numeric information such as data grouped into categories. In these cases, the mode illustrates the most frequently reported category.

Summary of Measures of Central Tendency

Measure of Central Tendency	What It Is	When It Should Be Used
MEAN	The average or midpoint in the range of a group of numbers	Can only be used on <u>numerical</u> data. It is a good descriptor of central tendency in non-skewed data distributions. For skewed distributions, it can be a useful descriptor of the degree of *skewedness* in the data (rather than central tendency), especially when it is compared to the median value.
MEDIAN	The middle number in a distribution of numbers, sorted from low to high	Can only be used on <u>ordinal</u> data (either numerical or categorical data with a natural order (e.g., Negative, Neutral, and Positive)). It is most useful for describing the central tendency in data that is skewed, or has extreme outlying values.
MODE	The most frequent value within a group of numbers	Most useful when examining categorical data to inform which values are most frequent.

MEASURES OF DISPERSION

WHEN REVIEWING MEASURES of central tendency it is important to understand how much variability there is between the numbers that make up the sample under study. In any group of numbers, measures of dispersion – or variability - help to describe the range over which numerical data are spread, and in essence how the values differ from one another. Measures of central tendency that provide information on where the middle of the range of numbers fall. The variance provides information about how the numbers fall around this central point.

While there are many different ways to describe dispersion, only two basic methods will be described here: numerical range and standard deviation.

RANGE. The simplest measure of dispersion is the *range*. The range represents the difference between the largest and the smallest numerical value in the distribution of data. The range may also be presented as (X,Y) where X is the smallest number and Y is the largest number. The range thus provides additional information about the extent or size of the interval between the lowest and highest numbers in the group under study.

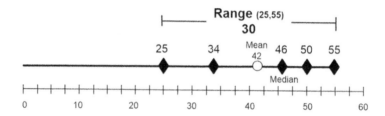

The range is often more informative when it is also presented along with the average or median values. This combination provides a more useful understanding of how the different measures fit together. However, the range is a somewhat limited measure of dispersion in that it does not describe how the data is distributed across the continuum in between the extreme values (high/low).

STANDARD DEVIATION/VARIANCE. The *variance* and *standard deviation* are two common methods for measuring the amount of dispersion or variation in the data around the mean value of a data distribution. The variance uses the sample size and how far each measure is from the mean to describe the dispersion. The larger the variance, the more the data is spread out around the mean point.

The standard deviation is a statistic that helps to make the concept of variance easier to understand. It is represented by the square root of the variance and expresses the amount of dispersion around the mean in the same unit as the measure that is being examined. For example, the standard deviation of a set of ages measured in "years," would also be expressed in the unit "years."

Standard deviations can be compared across data sets as long as the units are the same. For example, if the standard deviation of a second set of data on age is to be compared to the first data set on age discussed above, it would need to also be measured in years.

> **Note:** A video demonstration on how to calculate a standard deviation is presented in the on-line course entitled *Using Data as a Quality Tool in DD*. Readers who are interested in learning more about how to perform such a calculation are encouraged to access the on-line course available at: http://www.udiscovering.org.

RELATIVE NUMBERS: RATES AND PERCENTAGES

AT TIMES THE DATA that is typically used in I/DD programs can be presented as an *absolute* number (e.g., the number of cases, number of people with or without something). Other times data is better presented as a *percentage* or *rate*. A percentage or rate is a *relative* number, i.e., it reflects the relationship between the number of cases with or without something to the total number of cases in the population or sample from which the data was gathered. Converting data to rates often allows for more meaningful and accurate comparisons over time to illustrate trends or to identify differences that may be present between different groups (e.g., age groups, disability levels, types of service or support received, programs or state systems).

Absolute numbers (e.g., the actual number of cases) are useful when the size of the sample is the same over time. For example, if evaluating access to a specialized form of psychiatric care and there were 100 people reviewed in one year and 101 reviewed the next year, it would be appropriate to use the absolute number when comparing years. However, if the sample size differed, either over time or another independent variable (e.g., large vs. small private provider agency), the use of absolute numbers would be very misleading. Consider the following example: if in one year an organization sampled 100 people and 25 were found to have received the specialized care and in the second year the same organization only sampled 50 people and 20 were found to have received the service, the use of absolute numbers (25 vs. 20) would make it appear as though there was a reduction in service. In reality however, the relative percentage or rate of care actually improved (25% vs. 40%).

> **Special Consideration.** It is important to make sure that when absolute numbers are reported as the primary data in a comparative analysis that the size of the samples is the same or almost the same. If not, use relative numbers such as percentages or rates.

PERCENTAGES. Percentages are a very common relative numeric and are often found in data related to I/DD services and service systems. A percentage is equal to the number divided by the total X 100. For example, if 25 people out of 1000 received a specialized type of behavioral health care, a description using a percentage would indicate that special care was provided to 2.5% of the people reviewed (25/1000 X 100).

RATES. It is sometimes less useful to simply look at the number of events in a population that took place within a given period of time than it is to convert that information into a rate. Rates can be used to examine trends over time or to compare different groups of people. For example, when assessing the number of events in a population, a rate helps to standardize the data relative to the size of the population. This can lead to a more meaningful comparison for populations of different sizes or that vary a great deal over time.

A rate is actually just a fraction or ratio that uses a standard unit of measurement. For instance, when analyzing unusual incident data or other types of events that take place within a service system, the numerator is represented by the number of people who experienced the incident during a specified time period; the denominator is the number of people in the population under study in that same period of time. Rates are always expressed with a unit. For event rates, we typically use a unit of *people* such as incidents per 100 people, per 1,000 people or even per 100,000 people. When comparing rates, it is extremely important that the rates under study use the same unit.

$$\text{Event Rate} = \frac{\text{Number of Events}}{\text{Population}} \times \text{Unit}$$

Example: Assume an I/DD provider served an average of 500 adults (the population being analyzed) during the calendar year (time period) and 20 of those individuals went to the hospital emergency room during that year (numerator). The rate of emergency room visits (the event) per 100 people would be equal to:

$$\frac{20 \text{ Emergency Room Visits}}{500 \text{ People}} \times 100 \text{ People} = 4 \text{ Visits per 100 People}$$

Using this type of measure allows the provider organization to directly compare one year to another or compare itself to another organization of a different size.

> **Special Consideration.** The use of rates is usually a much more accurate and useful method for describing events/incidents, particularly when comparing across groups or time.

WHICH UNIT SHOULD BE USED

FOR VERY SMALL POPULATIONS, such as those that may be present within a small service provider or even a small state disability system that serves only a few thousand persons, the rate may be more useful if it is presented using a smaller reference unit, such as 100 people (e.g., 4 events per 100). However, when the population of persons served (denominator) is very large or when comparisons against the general population are going to be made, rates expressed as events per 100,000 people may be most appropriate. When determining which standard unit to use think about what will be most meaningful to your audience and whether or not you will be comparing your rates to existing benchmarks. Make sure you use the same standard throughout your analysis and reports to minimize confusion.

> **Additional Consideration.** When a rate is very low, such as often occurs when looking at rates of unusual or specific and rare events, it is usually easier to understand the rate if it is adjusted so that it is not presented as a small fraction of a "person." For example, rather than expressing a rate of motor vehicle accidents for persons with I/DD as 0.1 accidents per 100 people it is easier to understand the rate when expressed as 1 accident per 1,000 people.

CALCULATING AN EVENT RATE

> **Note:** The on-line course entitled *Using Data as a Quality Tool in DD* contains interactive practice examples for calculating event rates. These interactive tools are provided to enhance learning for interested users. Go to the following site to access the *Risk Management in DD* series of on-line courses; http://www.udiscovering.org.

WHEN CALCULATING A RATE it is important to make sure that everyone who is counted in the population (denominator) has the *potential* of being included in the numerator, i.e., the population should contain anyone who could have experienced the particular event and would have been counted in the numerator. This is an important consideration that is often overlooked. It is especially critical when there are a large number of "discharges" or other changes such as deaths or transfers in the total population served that take place during the time period under consideration.

TYPES OF RATES

THERE ARE THREE basic types of rates that can be used when analyzing and reporting most findings commonly computed in I/DD systems. These include crude and specific rates.

1. **Crude rate.** A crude rate represents the number of events in a population during a period of time divided by an estimate of the population during that same time period. Because populations of people served by an I/DD service system tend to change in size over time, an approximation of the population size is generally used to calculate rates. Two types of estimates that are commonly used for the population are an average over the time period or the size of the population at the midpoint of the time period (e.g.. mid-year for an annual rate). The rates calculated in the example presented above were crude rates.

> **CAUTION:** The use of a crude rate has important limitations. When using a crude rate it is important to remember that the rate is not corrected for underlying differences that affect the event (risk factors) in the populations. For example, different age distributions may change health-related events such as hospitalizations because the risk of certain health conditions increases with age.

2. **Specific rates.** One way to examine the potential effect of certain factors on the data is to use a specific rate. An age-specific rate is an example of a specific rate that is restricted to a particular age group, for example a group that is 45-54 years old. To calculate an age-specific rate, the number of events within the time period for people within the age group is divided by the average number of people in the age group during the time period. Remember that the population used to calculate the rate must have the *potential* of being included in the numerator.

$$\text{Event Rate for Ages 45-54} = \frac{\text{Number of Events in People aged 45-54}}{\text{Population of People aged 45-54}} \times \text{Unit}$$

Many different types of specific rates can be calculated, including those that are specific to age groups, gender, service locations, etc. In the calculation of a specific rate any restrictions used (e.g., females only) must be applied to <u>both</u> the numerator and the denominator.

3. **Adjusted rates.** Rates may be adjusted to estimate what the rate might be if a particular characteristic in a population were different. Risk adjusted rates, using factors like age, are a common type of adjusted rates and can be useful for understanding comparisons between different populations or data over time for a singular population where factors related to the outcome or event being measured differ. Examples may be mortality rates in a population that serves children and adults vs. one that only serves adults; or data from one year to the next after service eligibility rules change for the population. [More information about adjusted rates will be presented in a section on "risk adjustment."]

RELATIVE DESCRIPTIVE STATISTICS

When presenting data, it is often very informative to show how information categorized in one group relates to another. *Relative descriptive statistics* are used to accomplish this, i.e., to examine groups of data in relation to one another. For example, consider a set of data that contains information about different types of incidents that represent increased risk such as hospital emergency room visits, hospitalization admissions, involvement with law enforcement, etc. Rank ordering this type of data can identify which type of incident occurs most frequently.

RELATIVE RANKING. In relative ranking, categories of information are ranked in descending order by the number of times they appear in the data. Caution should be exercised when using relative rankings since it depends upon a number of factors that must be carefully controlled. Some more common examples of factors that can distort relative rankings include:

- **Standard definitions and categories:** The definitions for each of the categories that are included in the ranking must be exactly the same across any groups that are compared. For instance, what is reported as a "behavioral incident" by one agency must be the same as what is reported by another in order for them to be compared. Otherwise, if one agency includes many more types of events in their definition of "behavioral incidents" this could change the ranking expectations for that and other categories of incidents. This would cause relative ranking of the data to be potentially invalid and lead to erroneous conclusions when attempting to compare the two providers.

- **Variation in Other Categories:** The relative ranking of a category may vary over time, even though the number of times it appears in the data remains the same. This can occur if other categories around it change. This issue is not uncommon in I/DD service systems when reporting and demographic data systems undergo frequent changes and enhancements designed to improve the system. It is very important to exercise caution when comparing data that may have been recorded in a different system, time period or with different categorical definitions.

Therefore always consider a variety of factors that may influence or distort the use of rankings. When analyzing relative rankings, it is advisable to examine the category specific rates to understand more objectively how each of the various categories may have changed over time or across populations. If major changes in the relative rankings are present, always consider the possibility of bias due to the factors described above before concluding an observed difference is "real" and meaningful.

CAUTIONS WHEN USING DESCRIPTIVE STATISTICS

USE CAUTION WHEN first examining data, particularly if it suggests changes which do not make sense or that are very different from what was expected. The analysis may, in fact, be inaccurate; or the data may reflect an unanticipated artifact, including an insufficient and small sample size. Of course, the finding may be correct as well.

If the results of a descriptive data analysis vary widely from and do not "fit" with expectations one should review other relevant measures and associated indicators. When there is a large difference in data (e.g., a number of events) between groupings of service recipients or over time in one population, it is important to question whether or not it is a *significant* change or merely a reflection of a more normal and expected fluctuation. This issue is of particular importance in small populations typically seen in I/DD programs or systems and which often show more exaggerated fluctuations in measures, like rates, than are seen in larger populations. This difference is very often due to the bias that occurs when analyzing "small" numbers that can be dramatically influenced by tiny changes. Remember that unlike large population studies (e.g., those that are published by the federal government or can be found in large-scale research studies) much of the data analyzed by I/DD organizations represents a relatively small number of cases. The smaller the population or sample, the less likely differences will be statistically significant.[iv] Small numbers are very sensitive to changes in only a few cases, especially if there are extremes or "outliers" present in the data. Absent statistical significance, it is important to exercise caution when reviewing data and drawing conclusions. Therefore look for *convergence* of findings and other data that may help to confirm any conclusions you may be entertaining.

> **Special Consideration.** Take care when drawing conclusions from an analysis, particularly if it reflects a finding that is novel and/or substantially deviates from experience. Look for convergence of information that can support the result before finalizing "conclusions."

> **CAUTION.** When reviewing rates, it is especially important to recognize potential issues that may be related to the size of the underlying population. As a simple example, suppose an analysis shows that a provider has a rate of 1 motor vehicle accident per 100,000 people in a given year. In a population that contains 200,000 people, that translates to 2 people being involved in a motor vehicle accident. If we then find that the rate of accidents doubles in the following year, it would be relatively easy to conclude that a dramatic increase in accidents had taken place. In reality however, this new rate means that there were 4 accidents that year - out of 200,000 people – compared to 2 accidents the year before. This finding actually represents a relatively small change in a large population of 200,000 people.
>
> In contrast, consider a rate of 1 motor vehicle accident per 1,000 people for this same population in year one. This equals 200 motor vehicle accidents in the total population of 200,000. When the rate doubles the next year, the new rate would represent 400 motor vehicle accidents. In this case, the doubling of the rate does reflect a dramatic increase. Always pay attention to the size of the population when reviewing rates.

MAKING INFERENCES FROM DESCRIPTIVE STATISTICS

IN CONTRAST TO DESCRIPTIVE statistics, *inferential statistics* are useful for examining whether any observed difference between two sets of data is significant. In contrast to descriptive statistics, inferential statistics use tests and the concept of significance that allow one to draw conclusions based on the evidence presented by the data. Inferential statistics can be very helpful for identifying issues that may impact safety and quality of services and for validating findings from data analysis.

[iv] Statistical significance is an assessment of whether the sample reflects a pattern, e.g. the same results would be obtained over and over again if the same analysis were repeated using other samples of the population under study, or whether it is due to chance. It is determined using statistical distributions.

The term *significant* when used in this context basically means there is a reasonable amount of evidence that a real or actual difference exists, and that the observed difference is not due simply to chance or normal fluctuation in the variables under review. Additionally, significance can be used to help quantify the strength of the evidence. Significance is usually presented on a scale ranging from 0.0 to 1.0, or sometimes as a percent ranging from 0% to 100%. The level of significance represents how certain one can be that the analytic finding is not due to chance.

One of the more common cut-off points for determining significance with typical I/DD data is 0.05 or 5%. Test results that meet or are below this value are considered "significant." This level of significance means that the observed difference has enough evidence to suggest that the probability it is due to chance is 5% or less. In other words, one can be at least 95% certain that the difference is not due to chance and is instead real.

> **Special Consideration.** Before using inferential statistical tests, including the methods described in this book and the associated on-line course, it is strongly recommended that organizations consult a qualified statistician. While inferential statistics can be extremely useful as an analytic tool, they must be used appropriately. Each of the various statistical tests has different "assumptions" which the data must meet in order for these tests to be used in a valid fashion. One of the more important requirements is the presence of a large enough sample size. Consulting an expert in statistical analysis is one of the best methods for assuring proper use of inferential techniques.

Some of the more common tests that may be helpful in generating greater understanding of findings when analyzing data within an I/DD service organization include the Chi-square test (or Pearson Chi-square test) and the T-test (often referred to as the Student's T-test). A summary of each of these tests is presented below.

PEARSON CHI SQUARE TEST

MUCH OF THE DATA encountered in I/DD programs is organized into categories – such as the type of environment in which people live (e.g., large congregate care facilities, small community based residences, independent living, at home with family, etc.). For this type of data, there are different inferential statistical tests that can be used to help answer questions about differences that may exist between categories. One of the more common is the *Chi-square Test of Independence*. This test examines whether one factor is 'independent' of the other by examining whether observed patterns are the same across groups. This concept of *independence* means that the pattern that is observed for one factor is the same regardless of the value of the other factor.

An example would be testing whether the number of staff injuries in programs operated by a provider organization is *independent* of the gender of the staff person. If the pattern of injuries is the same for men as it is for women, the injuries would be considered to be *independent* of gender, i.e., not statistically different. This test is also useful for examining changes in a condition or variable (e.g., hospitalizations) that may take place from one year to the next, or across different populations.

Chi-square assesses whether there is statistically significant evidence that the pattern across the categories is truly different between the two groups (or is really due to chance or artifacts in measurement). To learn more about how to calculate and interpret the Chi-square test and review an example of its use see **Appendix H** (Examples for Using a Chi-square Test).

STUDENT'S T TEST

THE STUDENT'S T-TEST IS USED to examine whether or not the mean (average) of two sets of continuous data (such as age) are the same or are significantly different. It is <u>not</u> used for categorical data where the Chi-square test is more appropriate. For example, the Student's t-test would be used to answer a question such as: "*Is the mean age of people who had hospital emergency room visits in 2012 the same as the mean age of people who went to the ER in 2013?*" The t-test assesses whether there's enough evidence to suggest that there is a significant difference in the mean (average age) of the two groups. To learn more about how to calculate a Student T-test and review an example of its use, go to **Appendix I** (Example for Calculating Student's t-test).

There are a large assortment of statistical tests that can be performed on the many different types of data that are typically present in I/DD service systems. It is beyond the scope of this book and the associated on-line course to cover all of them or to provide detailed instruction in statistical analysis. For this reason, it is strongly recommended that organizations consult with an expert statistician when undertaking more complex and detailed data analysis. Doing so will better assure that the organization does not utilize the wrong methods and generate inaccurate findings that can ultimately result in inaccurate findings and adversely influence decisions that can impact the safety and quality of services.

RISK ADJUSTMENT: COMPARE "APPLES TO ORANGES"

WHEN EXAMINING DATA across years or between different populations, it is important to understand how certain characteristics of the population may affect the analytic results. One characteristic that can be extremely important, particularly for health-related data, is age. For example, age is the single largest predictor of mortality, and the patterns of certain medical issues such as chronic diseases and conditions can significantly change with age. Therefore when comparing data from two different groups, it is important to recognize, understand and examine the underlying age distribution of the different populations.

> **Special Consideration:** Think carefully about what special risk factors may be present within the populations of people served by an organization. When appropriate, issue cautionary notes regarding the limitations of the data analysis. When possible take the time to risk adjust and statistically test the data so that it can provide a more accurate picture of any meaningful differences that may exist.

In addition to age, other important "risk factors" that must be taken into consideration vary based on the type of information that is being analyzed. For incident data, factors such as the prevalence of chronic health conditions and co-morbidities, secondary disabilities - particularly those that may affect mobility; weight and healthy lifestyle behaviors such as smoking, diet and physical activity levels can all influence health-related incidents. Keep in mind that certain characteristics of the services provided by an organization may also result in different risk factors between segments of the population or in comparison to other populations. For example, if people who require more intensive medical care (such as in a nursing home) are discharged from a service population, then health-related incident patterns may look different (e.g., occur at lower rates) than for a population that serves people for the duration of their lifespan. In a similar fashion, programs that support people with special behavior management issues compared to services that do not will naturally show expected differences in the presence of psychotropic medication usage, physical intervention and even certain critical incidents. Caution therefore must always be exercised when conducting comparisons of this type of data.

NOTE: Information regarding special risk factors that are important considerations when providing support to persons with intellectual and developmental disabilities is presented in greater detail in both the book and associated on-line course entitled *Risk Screening in Developmental Disabilities,* available at; https://udiscovering.org.

STRATIFIED RATES

ONE SIMPLE WAY to examine the effect of a particular risk factor is to stratify the data. Stratification is the process of separating the values of one measure by the value of another. Rates can then be compared across the different levels of the risk factor, or strata, to see whether the rate of the outcome or measure changes.

For example, assume an agency serves a population of 375 people. It knows that 84.5% or 8.5 per 10 people received an annual physical exam in the past year. The agency would like to know if there's a difference in the rate of physical exams between people who can walk independently and those that require some assistance to ambulate. To examine this, the agency could stratify the annual physical exam data by the mobility status of its service recipients, as illustrated in the following table:

Mobility Status	No. People with Annual Physical Exam in Past Year	Total No. People Served	Rate of Annual Exams (per 10 people served)
Can walk independently	230	250	9.2
Needs assistance to walk	55	75	7.3
Uses a wheelchair	32	50	6.4
Total	317	375	8.5

69

The data in this example seems to indicate that the rates of receiving an annual physical exam differ by mobility status. As can be seen, 92% or 9.2 out of 10 of people served by the agency and who can walk independently received an annual physical exam in the last year. However, only 73% or 7.3 out of 10 people who need assistance to walk, and 64% or 6.4 out of 10 people who use a wheelchair received a physical exam. When comparing the population in terms of factors that may be influenced by mobility status (e.g., health indicators, falls, injuries) it may be appropriate to use stratified rates. This data also suggests that there may be a barrier to receiving an annual physical exam for people who require assistance with mobility, an issue that probably requires further examination and that the agency may wish to address in the future.

RISK ADJUSTED RATE

A RISK-ADJUSTED RATE estimates what the rate for the population would be if it had a different distribution of a target risk factor (the distribution of the population to which it is being adjusted). Risk-adjusted rates are useful when comparing mortality statistics across populations that may be different in terms of how the risk factor is distributed within the population (e.g., a comparison between a much older nursing home population and the general U.S. population). The rate is adjusted by weighting the numbers in each risk group to make the underlying distribution of the risk factor the same between two populations. For example, age-adjusted rates are commonly reported in national and public health mortality statistics and help in making more valid comparisons between mortality data from the I/DD field and population without disabilities benchmarks.

Appendix J (How to Calculate an Age-adjusted Rate) contains more detail and provides examples for risk adjusting I/DD data for age.

Chapter 8
Interpreting Results

MAKING SENSE OF DATA and the results of an analysis requires *critical thinking*. Such "thinking" is a process that requires one to:

- Ask questions and continually seek clarity about the data and findings
- Be logical and rational in how conclusions are arrived at
- Use objective evidence and avoid over reliance on anecdote and assumption
- Evaluate the validity and reliability of the data and information that is used
- Employ a systematic approach to the organization and use of data and its analysis

Critical thinking therefore entails independently questioning assumptions, assessing and analyzing information, and integrating data from various pathways to establish fact-based conclusions that can more effectively guide decision making. The concept of critical thinking has been described as:

"The ability to judge the plausibility of specific assertions, to weigh evidence, to assess the logical soundness of inferences, to construct counter-arguments and alternative hypotheses."[1]

In this book and its associated on-line course we focus on the type of data that most readers will traditionally find and use in an I/DD service system. Our evidence is, in part, the data that we've collected and analyzed over the years. However, it must be remembered that *evidence* is broader than just the data we collect. Evidence also comes in the form of context – what we "know" about the service system and the environment in which we've collected our data. It includes what we "know" about the strengths and weaknesses of our data, and how our system has changed and evolved over time. The people who analyze and use data in all organizations and systems that support people with intellectual and developmental disabilities must also adopt this perspective in order to promote the most effective use of objective information as they actively pursue quality and continuous improvement.

Activity: When starting to interpret a set of data or the results from a recent analysis, review the list of data qualities discussed in previous chapters and summarized in **Appendix B** (validity, comprehensiveness, etc.). Identify the strengths and weaknesses that are known to exist in the data. Think carefully about the assumptions that are being made about the qualities of the data. Ask whether or not such assumptions may be compromising the validity and integrity of the analytic findings. If they are, identify what could be done to reduce bias resulting from the major issues that have been identified.

Critical thinking requires that all of this evidence is put together in a thoughtful, reflective manner in order to guide decision-making. It requires asking probing questions about the data that will be used and the assumptions underlying that data. It also requires one to question whether or not the data makes sense when balanced against other evidence and experience. Balance is critical. Objective data and analyses are not intended to be viewed (and acted upon) in isolation. Instead, the results from data analyses should always be integrated and blended together with other sources of information to form a more complete and dynamic perspective of the issue being studied.

Critical thinking is therefore multidimensional in nature. It requires individuals and organizations to approach their understanding of services and supports from multiple perspectives. One way to help achieve this more integrated and holistic understanding is to ensure that people from different roles within an organization review and discuss the data, the analysis and resultant findings in an open, cooperative and collaborative fashion.

GENERAL RULES FOR REVIEWING DATA

WHILE THE CONSISTENT use of objective data can be a valuable tool in understanding and managing the quality of services, it is important to remember that it is not "perfect." Data and the results from structured analysis must be used in an intelligent and cautious fashion. As noted, it is extremely important to seek balance between data and other sources of information and to avoid "jumping to conclusions." In other words, always approach the review of data with a "questioning" mind. Some general rules when reviewing data include:

ALWAYS:
- Analyze the analysis
- Identify major issues that may compromise the data.
- Do not generalize the findings beyond their limits.
- Balance the review. The data is one point of reference – take into consideration other sources of information and experience.

NEVER:
- Make assumptions about the data – ask questions.
- Expand the findings to an entire population or system – unless it is appropriate.
- Treat the data as "significant" unless it says it is.
- Jump to conclusions without checking other sources.

> **Special Consideration:** Be careful not to over-interpret data. Use the data to suggest questions for further examination. Try not to jump to conclusions, and use multiple sources of information where possible to guide action.

UNDERSTANDING OBSERVED DIFFERENCES

WHEN REVIEWING THE RESULTS of data analysis, it is important to thoroughly examine and understand *observed differences*. This can be accomplished using inferential statistics, as reviewed in the previous chapter. Inferential statistical tests, revealing the presence or absence of statistical significance, can greatly aid in understanding how much evidence in analytic findings is due to chance or reflects a real difference in the data. But, while these tests can measure the amount of evidence, they <u>cannot</u> inform the quality of that evidence.

To assess the quality of the data, critical thinking skills must be applied. The following sections in this chapter focus on how to identify what is "driving" any observed difference and whether or not this "driver" is an artifact of how the data was collected or analyzed, or whether it is "real."

WHAT'S DRIVING THE DIFFERENCE? When significant differences or probable trends are observed one should ask: *"What is driving the difference?"* According to epidemiological experts[2] there are two major issues we should consider when addressing the question *"Are the drivers real or are they artifactual?"*

- *Artifactual* effects are the result of changes that are made in how we count, categorize, collect or include or exclude certain information and data. These effects create differences that are not an actual reflection of what is happening, but rather result from what and how we measure something. Artifactual effects are important to take into consideration since they can suggest that differences exist where there really are none. They can also mask true differences and trends when they are, in fact, present.

  In the field of I/DD, how one defines a population, what periods of time are used for the analysis, what type of information is collected, how that information is collected, and other such variables are all potential artifactual effects that can bias findings and lead to faulty conclusions. It is essential for individuals who will be analyzing and using data to pay special attention to these issues and carefully control them whenever possible.

- In contrast, *real* differences are due to actual changes in the population or system under study. Real differences can be driven by systemic factors such as the quality of supports and services, organizational factors such as policies and practices, or even individual-level factors such as the health status or the presence of certain health conditions within a given population. It is important to understand when and where these effects exist and how they may be influencing the data that is being reviewed and analyzed. Inattention to such real differences can bias findings and lead to incorrect conclusions. Proper attention to observed real differences can help guide the recognition of a need for prompt intervention and longer term preventive action that will improve the safety and quality of services provided by an organization.

As noted, artifactual effects such as changes in the quality of data - and even in how information is categorized for purposes of reporting - can suggest differences where none actually exist. The following example illustrates how artifactual effects can influence the measurement of reported critical incidents and consequently lead to questionable findings in an I/DD service system.

Example 1: Errors in the count of events or occurrences. Artifactual errors can affect the *numerator* that is used to calculate a rate. For example, assume the numerator represents the number of events (critical incidents that are reported). When faulty or erroneous measurement (i.e., reporting) reduces the number of events that are recorded, this error directly leads to the calculation of a reduced event rate. In a similar fashion, if the artifact increases the count of events (i.e., numerator is too big), this error in reporting increases the event rate, as illustrated below:

EXAMPLE 1: Error in the count of events.

IF the **Actual Number** of Incidents was 160, the **Real Incident Rate** would be:

$$\frac{160 \text{ Incidents Reported}}{1000 \text{ People}} \quad X \ 100 = \quad \textbf{16} \text{ Incidents per 100 People}$$

Artifactual Effect from **Under-reporting**:

$$\frac{120 \text{ Incidents Reported}}{1000 \text{ People}} \quad X \ 100 = \quad \textbf{12} \text{ Incidents per 100 People}$$

Artifactual Effect from **Over-reporting:**

$$\frac{250 \text{ Incidents Reported}}{1000 \text{ People}} \quad X \ 100 = \quad \textbf{25} \text{ Incidents per 100 People}$$

Some common artifactual errors in I/DD systems data that occur rather often include:

- **Changes in accuracy of reporting events:** When a reportable event takes place but is not recorded and therefore not included in the analyses, the omission will artificially deflate the event rate. When first starting a reporting/monitoring system or when implementing major changes to an existing system, the quality of the early data will often be lower than is desired. New and unfamiliar monitoring systems may not capture all events. When the accuracy of the reporting system is improved over time, it can result in findings that look like there has been an increase in events. This apparent "increase" is really just an artifact of improvements in the collection of data and is not necessary a result of a real increase in events. When present, it is extremely important to highlight this possibility when reporting results.

- **Changes in rules/procedures of classification:** This type of effect is related to how events or other types of data are categorized (e.g., when labeling service lines or types of residential support). Changes in what categories are used or in how cases are assigned to different categories will result in unintended errors in the analyses and resultant findings. For example, it is not unusual in new reporting systems to have more "unknown" or "undetermined" entries for certain data fields. Over time, and as methods are adjusted to provide information more consistently this tends to change. As reporting systems mature and there is an improvement in the quality of information, it is therefore not unusual to find an increase in certain categories of data that are recorded. This may lead to a decrease in reported events within other categories. The resulting change is simply a reflection of the availability of more detailed and accurate information, clarification of "rules" and experience by reporters. The changes over time are an artifactual effect, not a real change in the number of actual events.

Individuals who are responsible for collecting, organizing and analyzing data must use care to identify the presence of these types of common artifactual effects. If present and not adequately addressed, they can lead to a variety of inaccurate conclusions and both waste resources and drive ineffective efforts to improve service quality fostering a focus on the wrong "problem."

To help identify potential artifactual effects in many forms of I/DD system data, consider asking and then answering the following questions:

1. *"Were there recent system changes that may have resulted in differences in how data is reported?"* Examples include implementation of new policies or procedures, additional or different training in reporting or the collection of information, changes in requirements for information collection in settings outside of an organization's direct control (e.g., living at home, schools, long-term care), instituting a new electronic data/reporting system, putting in place new or revised formats for reporting, publicity regarding the importance of reporting, etc.

2. *"Have there been changes in how information is categorized?"* Examples include modification in categories of information, inclusion of a new service line in affecting who is counted in the data, changes in how an organization groups residential or day support services, changes in labels or names for sub-groups within a service type, consolidations or mergers of programs, etc.

3. *"Has there been a change in the source of information bring used in the analysis?"* Examples include new or different requirements for external reporting on a subgroup of people (e.g., . hospitalization of people 30 days after they leave a service system), use of another group's/agency's information collection tool, changes in how data from external sources is incorporated, etc.

Example 2: Errors in population counts. Artifactual effects in population counts can also cause inaccuracies in rates and mask true differences that take place over time or that exist between different groups. These errors affect the *denominator* of an event rate. In other words, when the artifact *reduces* the number of people counted in the population, it will *increase* the event rate. Similarly, if the artifact increases number of people counted in the population, it will automatically decrease the event rate. Artificial changes to the population number that is used to calculate the event rate will also lead to false conclusions and result in resource inefficiencies as an organization chases after a "problem" that may not, in effect, really exist. – or, fail to identify one that does.

To guard against bias that results from this type of artifactual effect, it can help to ask the following types of questions before beginning extensive analysis:

1. *"Were there recent system changes that may have resulted in a change of data quality affecting the accuracy of population counts?"* Examples can include the implementation of a new or revised client data system, acquisition and use of new technology that improves the reliability, validity and/or timeliness of data recording and collection, better orientation and training for

personnel responsible for inputting data, changes in staff responsibility for maintaining service recipient records, etc.

2. *"Does the data accurately capture information on everyone who should be included?"* Examples include situations where the denominator in an analysis does not include persons who have been transferred to another system although the organization continues to receive event reports about these individuals; the denominator includes everyone the organization serves but information is not collected for individuals who receive only intermittent support.

EXAMPLE 2: Error in population count:.

IF the **Actual Size** of the population was 1000 People, the **Real Incident Rate** would be:

$$\frac{\text{160 Incidents Reported}}{\text{1000 People}} \quad \text{X } 100 = \quad \textbf{16 } \text{Incidents per 100 People}$$

Artifactual Effect from **Under-estimating** the Population:

$$\frac{\text{160 Incidents Reported}}{\text{800 People}} \quad \text{X } 100 = \quad \textbf{20 } \text{Incidents per 100 People}$$

Artifactual Effect from **Over-estimating** the Population:

$$\frac{\text{160 Incidents Reported}}{\text{1200 People}} \quad \text{X } 100 = \quad \textbf{13 } \text{Incidents per 100 People}$$

Remember that the population included in an analysis should reflect everyone who could be captured with the event reporting under consideration. It should not incorporate those persons who would not be included for reporting. Special attention to this issue should be given to analyses that examine change over time as it is somewhat common to experience subtle and even major changes in the demographics and the size of the population that is captured in I/DD data systems. These changes can and most likely will result in unintended errors when analyzing the data.

PRECAUTIONS WHEN ANALYZING TRENDS OVER TIME

SERVICE ORGANIZATIONS and public oversight systems that support people with I/DD very often want to compare data from one time period to the next (e.g., include comparison data in annual reports). When reviewing statistics across multiple time periods it's important to identify any substantial changes in the distribution of variables that may bias the data and to either correct for these changes or to highlight their potential impact on the analysis. Common examples include:

- Changes in eligibility requirements (e.g., age, disability categories)

- Program or facility closures or changes to the type of supports provided
- Geographic or service system reorganizations
- Rates of illness (e.g., influenza pandemics) for health-related measures or presence of significant natural disasters
- General demographic shifts (e.g. gross population change from the migration of living individuals between age groups)

> **Special Consideration:** Be careful that major changes have not taken place in a service system, or in reporting requirements, the population that is served by the organization, or in risk factors that may impact the analysis whenever analyzing statistics across multiple years.

HOW TO HANDLE ARTIFACTUAL DIFFERENCES. When artifactual effects are present it is often not possible to clearly discern how much impact they may have relative to the real cause of an observed difference, i.e., how much is due to the artifactual effect and how much is due to some true effect in the observed data. When this occurs it is extremely important to make sure those who use the data understand its potential limitations and the need to exercise care before making major decisions. Sometimes it may be more prudent to delay action temporarily in order to secure additional information and expand the data (e.g., allow additional time to elapse before reanalyzing the data). This can help determine if an observed trend is real or artifactual. In other cases, one may need to act right away in order to protect people from harm while seeking confirmation and additional data. The potential for harm (impact) and degree of risk that is associated with the factors under consideration will determine which strategy is most appropriate. In either case, further analysis and additional data will usually be warranted.

> **Special Consideration:** Whenever reporting data that is suggestive of trends, patterns or other issues that are suspect, make sure you identify and discuss possible artifactual effects to highlight the need for caution in reviewing the data.

CRITICAL EVALUATION OF FINDINGS

A CRITICAL EVALUATION of the results of data analysis inevitably circles back to asking key questions. It is important to always start with the purpose of your analysis, i.e., the question that were the focus of the analysis in the first place. Review how well the available data and process of analysis answer those questions. Next, take time to ask a series of follow-up questions that can help to validate findings:

- *Are these results what was expected?*
- *Does the pattern being observed make sense?*
- *Are there any artifacts that could be adversely influencing the results?*
- *Do other sources of information show agreement with these results?*

Finally, integrate the results from the analysis of data with other information to form a more complete picture. Look for a convergence of data and findings, i.e., evidence from different sources of information that all suggest a similar conclusion. For a more complete and accurate picture of a service delivery system, always aim to pull information together from various perspectives and different types of data (e.g., use service, process and outcome measurement data when available).

The following examples illustrate a few common situations where the use of multiple sources of information provide a more complete picture of the strengths and weaknesses that can exist in an I/DD service organization.

1. An agency measures the timeliness of annual service planning, and finds that it has a high rate of completing plans on time. However, a survey of participants reports a high rate of unmet need, indicating that while the process may be completed on time, there may be problems with the quality and/or adequacy of the plans or their implementation.

2. A public service system completes a new training initiative and qualification process for service providers related to the management of diabetes. The training rate among providers is high, and the majority of providers are able to meet the new qualifications within set timeframes. However, an examination of avoidable hospitalizations for short-term complications of diabetes in the following year shows that hospitalizations experienced an increase compared to pre-training levels.

3. An agency demonstrates high rates of compliance with required staff training regarding signs and symptoms of illness. However, an internal review shows a number of critical incidents involving the late recognition of signs and symptoms of illness and a corresponding delay in seeking treatment. Further review also shows a higher than normal rate of staff turnover at locations with high rates of these reported incidents, suggesting that initial training may not be providing knowledge and skill acquisition in symptom recognition.

4. A large service provider with multiple locations has been monitoring errors in medication administration for many years. Recently, the overall rate of errors has shown a statistically significant drop. Further review of the data shows that the number of errors has fallen to zero for three locations that historically had an average of 5 or more errors per month. All three of these locations recently acquired new staff that attended the same training sessions. Further review suggests that confusion and misunderstanding about reporting compliance was a possible cause for the drop in the rate, rather than an actual decrease in the number of medication errors. Note that very low rates for certain types of incidents or sudden decreases can be signs of reporting issues, not necessarily an improvement in the quality of service.

Activity: Think back to a recent set of data that has been examined, or one that is being considered for future review. Identify other sources of information that could be used to compare the findings to in order to gain another perspective. Are there other sources of information and evidence that could enhance the understanding of findings?

USE COMPARATIVE BENCHMARKS

BEFORE DRAWING MEANINGFUL conclusions from data, it is often important to understand whether or not findings are similar to or different from those present in similar populations and/or service systems. It can also be extremely useful to relate findings to goals that have established by the organization. This process of comparing findings from one system to another or to an established goal or target is termed *benchmarking*.

Benchmarking uses external sources of information as a comparison point of reference for a data set. Benchmarking can have great utility as a way to understand whether or not an organization's data shows "expected" patterns or is substantially different from that of the comparison group. Benchmarks can also help an organization establish targets and goals.

The use of objective benchmarks, when done appropriately, can prove valuable for enhancing understanding about the strengths and weaknesses within a service system to better enable the system to establish focused targets for quality improvement. However, benchmarking must be done with extreme caution to ensure that the comparison data is valid. If comparison groups are not selected appropriately, or are not properly risk adjusted, one can end up with faulty and extremely inaccurate conclusions.

The information from benchmarking is but one method for providing insight into what data may be revealing. Benchmarking should always be used in concert with other sources of information to foster a more complete – and accurate - understanding.

In order to most effectively use benchmarks, it is recommended that the following series of steps be utilized:

1. **Understand the data.** As noted earlier, it is important to assess the data that will be used by the organization to assure it is accurate, valid, reliable and useful. One should also evaluate the processes that have been used to collect the information. Understanding the limitations of the organization's own data is an essential first step for making valid comparisons with other sources of information.

2. **Understand the source of the benchmark.** If benchmark data will be used from another system, understand how the information was collected. Review whether or not the process is similar or substantially different from the methods used by an organization. Evaluate whether or not known differences can affect the meaning of the data and use it for comparison purposes. This is especially important in the field of I/DD since there are no clear standards or conventions that are yet available for creating valid comparative benchmarks.

3. **Evaluate the relevancy of the data.** If comparing data to an established goal, it is important to understand how and why the goal was established (i.e., it's aim). Of particular importance is evaluating whether or not the goal was designed specifically for the type of service system or population supported by the organization. In other words, evaluate how relevant the goal is to the data that will be used.

4. **Compare the organization's data to the benchmark.** When comparing data to the benchmark, take special care to ensure that all the data being reviewed is aligned as closely as possible to the benchmark. Always assess how the different data was measured (if

different methods are used, the comparison may not be valid). Look at how the variables were defined since it is not uncommon for different organizations and I/DD service systems to have unique ways of categorizing people and defining events. Consider using statistical tests, where possible, to assess the significance of observed differences. The use of such tests can help validate the appropriateness of using different comparison groups.

5. **Plan next steps.** Review whether the comparison data provides sufficient information to answer the target question. Where possible, use multiple measures to develop a complete understanding of the results of an analysis.

SELECT APPROPRIATE BENCHMARKS

SOMETIMES BENCHMARKS are chosen because they represent an ideal or desired and high state of performance. Other times, they're selected as examples of what may be 'typical' or 'normal' for a service system or program. While it is usually desirable to select benchmarks from within one's own field (e.g., another I/DD service system or organization), at other times it may be more useful to look outside of the disability arena for benchmarks. This can be most appropriate when:

- Benchmarks in comparison groups in the field of I/DD are not available or appropriate;
- The "measures' that are being considered can be expected to be similar across fields (e.g. the frequency of hospital visits).

Benchmarks may be used as best practice metrics or even to represent the extremes of a goal (e.g., a community-based I/DD program an organization operates might be expected to have fewer deaths than a nursing home setting due to differences in the underlying mortality risks associated with age and health status). However used, it is extremely important to understand why a particular data set is being selected for use as a benchmark and to remember that the utility of any benchmark data is highly dependent on the appropriateness of the comparison between two or more groups. The selection of benchmarks should always strive to minimize bias. When comparing an organization's data to other populations, the ideal benchmark is one that:

- Has similar demographics to the organization's population or sample, especially with regard to age, type and level of disability, eligibility requirements and service and support lines that are included in the comparison data.
- Uses data recording, analysis and reporting methods that are as close as possible to the methods used by the organization.

Benchmarking data is most appropriate and valid when it is the same as or very similar to the data that is being reviewed. Therefore, when selecting benchmarks, it is critical to avoid data comparisons that will increase artifactual differences due to population and methodology differences. When such differences are present, make sure to highlight them to assure readers are aware of any major limitations that are present. To help guide in the selection of appropriate benchmark data in I/DD organizations and service systems, it is recommended that the following questions be carefully considered:

- *How is the population included in the benchmark data different from the data that is being reviewed?*
- *Are there substantial differences in the distribution of age and risk factors related to it being measured?*

- *Does the comparison group have a very different age distribution, proportion of people with different types of health-related disabilities or very different service needs?*
- *Could any such difference affect the risk of an outcome being measured?*
- *If these differences do exist, how might they compromise or influence any comparison?*
- *Do the differences in risk factors increase or decrease the expectation of rates compared to the population being evaluated by the organization?*
- *Were different methods used to calculate the reported statistics (e.g., how rates were determined, categorization methods for including/excluding subpopulations, etc.)*
- *Was the source of information different, and if so, how?*

It may not be possible to answer all of these questions or to accurately predict how any identified differences might affect the statistics and therefore the validity of the data as an accurate benchmark. That is acceptable (and probably will be rather common when working with data in the field of I/DD). However, when potential bias is recognized and one is uncertain as to its impact, make sure to note the differences and instruct the audience (those who will be using the data) to exercise caution when conducting comparisons and to avoid "jumping" to conclusions.

CONSIDERATIONS FOR I/DD BENCHMARKS

DIFFERENT TYPES OF BENCHMARKS will often have different types of concerns that should be considered when determining their applicability to your I/DD system data. In this regard, the validity of potential benchmarks can be impacted by any of the following issues:

- **Related disability populations.** Statistics from other populations of people with varying forms of I/DD may be among the most helpful and directly comparable data to use as benchmarks for an I/DD organization or large service system. Unfortunately, the availability of this data is quite limited and there are important aspects related to how the specific comparative population is defined that can cause substantial artifactual differences. Always take into consideration:
  - o **Age.** Some I/DD service populations only include adults, whereas others include people that are served and supported across a lifespan (childhood through old age). Age differences can significantly impact certain types of data (e.g., health and mortality). Be careful when selecting comparison groups.
  - o **Disability eligibility.** The eligibility criteria (e.g., type and/or level of disability, health status and daily support needs) may differ across I/DD systems. Some systems only serve people with intellectual disabilities; others serve persons with ID and those with an autism spectrum disorder. Still others serve all persons with a defined developmental disability. Make sure comparisons are for similar disability groupings.
  - o **Selective subsets for incident/event reporting.** Some systems only report on incidents that occur within licensed or funded programs; some report on all persons enrolled in a system; others use a variety of different subsets of incidents for different groups of their service population. Understand who is included and who is excluded.

- ○ **Detail of the data collected.** Some system reports use data that is based on a minimal set of descriptive data or limited categories whereas other systems may use more detailed and multiple data sources to gather richer information. The use of different sources for the data may change how it is categorized and reported.

- **State laws.** The information available to a system for analysis and reporting can differ based on the requirements of state laws or other legal and policy restrictions. The basis for the data must therefore be carefully identified as it may under or over-represent the actual values within the population that is represented by the benchmark.

- **General population.** Conducting valid comparisons to statistics from the general population can be extremely complex. Some of the more important differences between the I/DD and general population that should always be considered include:

  - ○ **Age.** Very often, statistics within the general population have a different age distribution than that found in public and private organizations and systems that support people with I/DD. If the data is not presented in age groupings that allow easy identification of this distribution, there is a strong potential for artifactual effects that can render the comparison invalid.

  - ○ **Etiology and co-morbidity.** The risk of certain events and outcomes associated with special co-morbid conditions that are more common in persons with I/DD and the underlying etiologies of specific disabilities or syndromes can dramatically change population-level health, activity and survival expectations.

  - ○ **Risk profiles.** Health and incident/event related statistics for the general population are likely to differ due to difference in risk profiles. The general population may, for instance, have more injuries related to occupational causes, motor vehicle accidents, and risky behaviors such as those related to substance abuse and firearms. On the other hand, people with I/DD more often have a higher incidence of injuries due to a variety of health and behavior related issues such as aspiration, choking and falls.

Caution therefore should always be taken when using general population benchmarks. Make sure to take into consideration the issues reviewed above when interpreting the results of any comparative analysis. This is not to suggest that such benchmarking is to be avoided. On the contrary, it is an extremely useful tool that can be of great help in analyzing I/DD-based information and in providing important context for the results of your analysis. Just make sure to use benchmarks with appropriate prudence, and always note special considerations for those who will be reviewing and using the results of the data analysis.

USING BENCHMARKS

AS NOTED, EXTERNAL BENCHMARKS should be used as a very general guide for understanding findings from the analysis of data. They may be particularly helpful when reviewing information and the results of an analysis that has been performed for the first time or when historic data is not available. It is recommended that multiple sources of external benchmarks are used when possible. This will help provide a range within which one may expect the data to fall, and can help minimize the effect of specific differences between a service system or population and another reference source of data. When multiple sources of information converge and show the same pattern, it is much more likely to be an 'expected' pattern than one based upon a single data source. When differences between the data source(s) are known, especially when they are theorized to affect the validity of the comparison, remember to clearly state these differences.

EXAMPLE

FOR PURPOSES OF THIS EXAMPLE assume an organization's mortality data shows mortality rates that substantially differ based on the type of residential setting. This variation appears to make sense in that such differences in mortality between residential settings probably most likely vary based upon the needs of the individuals served within the residences. Such needs are often related to health conditions that most likely affect the risk of mortality. Comparing the pattern of mortality to another I/DD system can help to inform whether or not the differences observed in the agency show a pattern that can be expected, or one that differs from normal expectations.

However, when looking at the comparative data that is available, it is noted that the organization's service system data only includes adults while the comparative data from the other system includes both adults and children. Since it can be expected that the mortality rates would normally be lower for the system that includes children it is important to highlight this difference when reporting the results of the data analysis.

In fact, careful review of the data shows that while there are differences in the mortality rates by setting, the overall pattern is the same between the two systems. The mortality rate is lowest for people who live at home with family or independently. The rate is then higher for people who live in community group homes, and even higher for people in intermediate care facilities. The rate is the highest for people in nursing facilities. The change in magnitude in the rates is similar across the settings. In this instance, the use of a comparative benchmark, although not perfect, is able to demonstrate a pattern that strengthens the initial conclusion that there is an expected relationship between mortality and residential setting. Data from this example is presented in the table and graphs that follow.

Sample Comparison of Mortality Rates by Residential Setting

Type of Residential Support	Mortality Rate Per 1,000 People	
	System 1 (Adults Only)	System 2 (All Ages)
At Home/Family, Independent & Supported Living	7.6	7.2
Community Group Home, Community Training Home	22.9	14.5
Facility, ICF/MR	40.2	31.9
Nursing Facility	124.7	141.6

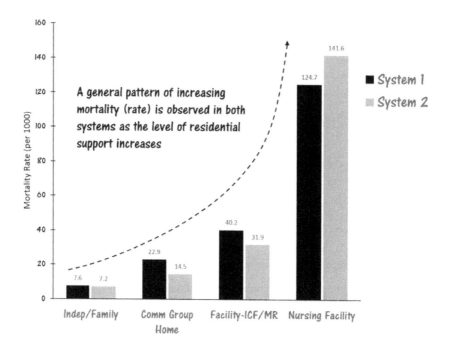

A general pattern of increasing mortality (rate) is observed in both systems as the level of residential support increases

WHERE TO FIND BENCHMARKS

THERE HAS BEEN A HISTORICAL dearth of directly comparable benchmarks available for use by organizations that serve people with I/DD. Increasingly, however, state I/DD systems have begun to make reports on individual outcomes and system performance publicly available on their websites and national initiatives such as the Core Indicators[3] project are evolving into useful resources for comparative benchmarks. Identifying and using appropriate comparative benchmarks can still be quite difficult and wrought with often subtle complications. There are too many variations that are utilized when reporting data in the field. Available reports may not provide sufficient information about the collection of the data. This inhibits the ability to appreciate whether or not the data can be appropriately compared to the organization's data.

This absence of conventions and standard approaches to the reporting of data within the field of I/DD complicates the selection and use of valid benchmarks. Therefore, when and if substantial differences appear to exist, care must be taken when communicating the data in formats such as tables or graphs that are often quickly referenced by readers. Rather, it can be more helpful to readers to present comparison data in narrative formats that can provide a more thorough explanation of any special considerations that readers need to take into account.

Some useful sources of information that can be used to generate benchmarks for I/DD data are summarized below. Data from these resources should always be used with due diligence and an appreciation for the special considerations reviewed above. It should also be noted that many new sources of data and potential benchmarks are constantly evolving and being added to the resources that can be used to evaluate the safety and quality of I/DD services and supports. Periodic internet searches are therefore strongly recommended.

Sample Resources for I/DD Benchmarks

Source	Description and Uses
STATE I/DD SYSTEMS AND PROVIDERS.	Most state agencies and large private organizations that provide or oversee supports and services for persons with developmental disabilities post reports and data on their internet sites. Some of this data can be used to generate benchmarks. To access this type of data, go directly to state or provider websites. It is strongly recommended that potential users peruse these sites to identify and evaluate the appropriateness of reported data for use as benchmarks (the sites are not listed here since they are undergoing constant updating and change). A review of data from outside an organization can provide rich insight into the organization's service quality and help target areas where closer examination is needed. When using other system data for benchmarking, use care and practice the cautions that have been reviewed above.
NATIONAL CORE INDICATORS[3]	The National Core Indicators (NCI) is a source of data that is voluntarily collected by public developmental disabilities agencies in order to measure and track their own performance. A standard set of indicators and processes are used across each state in order to generate comparable measures, using the same methods of data collection. Data is gathered through surveys to people with I/DD that receive state services and their families. The information collected covers areas deemed important by service recipients, providers of support and public agencies responsible for the oversight of I/DD service systems. It includes measures of system performance, staff stability, individual outcomes, family indicators and health, welfare and rights. The data is publicly available at both the national and state levels and can be very useful for establishing comparative and goal-oriented benchmarks.
KAISER FAMILY STATE HEALTH FACTS[4]	A State Health Facts website is operated by the Henry J. Kaiser Family Foundation that provides free access to health data on all 50 states. It includes data on more than 500 health topics, many of which may be of interest to I/DD service organizations. Data is collected from a variety of public and private sources, including: original Kaiser Family Foundation reports, data from public websites, and information purchased from private organizations. This information can be helpful when reviewing health related data. General population benchmarks like these must be used very carefully. Think about whether or not there is a reasonable expectation for similarities between the population of people supported by the I/DD organization and the general public.
HEALTHY PEOPLE 2020[5]	*Healthy People* is a federal initiative that provides science-based, 10-year national objectives for improving the health of all Americans. The program has collected data and provided informed targets for the last three decades. The objectives tend to focus on modifiable health outcomes, and can have great utility for both identifying comparison data, but also in goal setting. Each objective provides an overview with the rationale for the objective, and relevant information on the topic. As additional information is collected each year, it is updated on the website to show national progress toward the goal. If you use data from Healthy People 2020 as a benchmark for an I/DD population, make sure you align the age ranges.

BENCHMARK EXAMPLES

TWO EXAMPLES of benchmarks relevant for I/DD service systems are presented below to illustrate how the addition of context can affect conclusions drawn from the analysis of data.

Example 1: Influenza Deaths. In this example, an annual mortality report for a state disability agency examined the causes of death each year in a population of people with I/DD. In 2008, an increase was observed in the number of deaths due to influenza and pneumonia compared to previous years. In fact, the rate of death from these causes nearly doubled from the previous year. Usually a finding such as this would immediately suggest the need for further investigation to identify patterns that may be related to influenza and pneumonia in the living population. However, benchmark data was collected to provide context by looking at mortality rates in the general population. A review of such data indicated that the United States experienced a flu epidemic in 2008. Further investigation showed that the epidemic was seen locally in the state where the I/DD service system is based. It revealed a 400% increase in influenza diagnoses from the previous year.[6] The addition of this information provided an important context for understanding the two fold increase in deaths due to influenza and pneumonia within the I/DD system.

Example 2: Understanding Hospice Use. In this second example, a state disability service organization's mortality review committee observed that a small group of deaths of service recipients with terminal conditions were administered aggressive treatment options when hospice services should have perhaps been considered instead. The agency decided to look more carefully at the use of hospice for decedents that had been served by the agency.

- **Benchmark:** In the absence of any historical data, the first year of data reviewed by the committee was compared to the general population – both state and national rates. The agency found that hospice was used at a much lower rate within their agency than for the general population within the same state. Given that people with I/DD tend to die from more chronic and terminal conditions, the committee theorized that the rate of hospice use should probably be similar to if not higher than that of the general population.

- **More Information:** The state I/DD agency amended their mortality reporting form and health care record so it would ask additional questions about hospice. They also surveyed agency nurses to learn more about factors involved in the use of hospice. The agency learned that there was an apparent lack of awareness of existing hospice options by many support staff and confusion about the I/DD service system within hospice agencies. In addition, it appeared that there were existing policy barriers that were preventing the use of hospice services in certain supported residential settings.

- **System improvement:** The agency then engaged in an educational campaign with hospice providers and I/DD private providers within the state system. In addition, the agency modified policies and protocols to reduce identified barriers that were preventing the use of in-home hospice services.

- **Continued monitoring:** The agency monitored the use of hospice for a period of time and found the rate of use increased by 10% within three years. Upon follow-up, the use of hospice was found to align more closely with the rate found within the general population.

As these examples illustrate, the use of benchmark data can provide useful context. It can help an organization and other users of the data better understand findings from an analysis and answer the question *"So, what does this finding really mean?"* The establishing of such context can then help direct follow-up activity and the development of more meaningful quality improvement targets.

Chapter 9
Using Results

THE ABILITY of an organization to effectively communicate and actually use the result of data analysis is as important as is the collection and proper analysis of the data itself. If it isn't going to be used, why bother collecting it? All too often too much time and effort is placed on generating data that is ultimately not shared or ends up published in reports that no one reads or uses (i.e., reports that "gather dust" on book shelves or are filed away in the organization's archives). This phenomenon represents a tremendous waste of resource. It can negatively impact stakeholder interest in and motivation to report and review data, and it reduces the likelihood of the organization using objective information to identify and prevent safety hazards and improve the quality of its services and supports. To be truly effective the results of data analysis must be actively communicated and continuously used!

PRINCIPLES FOR PRESENTING DATA

WHEN PREPARING to communicate findings from data analyses adherence to the following principles can help to maximize the reader's appreciation for and understanding of the information:

1. **SIMPLICITY.** Keep it simple. It is very important to know your audience and what their proficiency may be in understanding and interpreting data. In many I/DD organizations the people who will be reading and using data reports do not have a very sophisticated knowledge about and understanding of data and statistical analysis. Therefore when preparing reports, it is important to provide clear, concise and simple data and the interpretation of findings. More complex and detailed analyses can be attached to reports as addendums (or links when using electronic reports). To accomplish this, try to:

   - Avoid "clutter" and limit the amount of information presented on tables, graphs or in narrative
   - Use engaging graphs that include only a few variables at a time
   - Incorporate visual symbols where relevant (e.g., arrows, +/- signs, colors) to represent findings in terms of type and direction of change
   - Explain statistical "significance" when presented (remember: many readers do NOT understand the concept or assume it means "importance").

2. **HIGHLIGHT.** Make it easy for the audience to identify the most important 'take away' points. Draw attention to "unusual" or statistically "significant" findings. Make important points "jump out" so that the reader will be able to focus on the most critical message. Try not to rely on numerous links to voluminous and separate documents or include a large number of footnotes/endnotes with dense and technical language that can distract the reader from grasping the most essential information. To help readers focus on what is most important, highlight key findings by incorporating:

- Face sheets or very brief executive summaries for your report with notations such as *"Pay Special Attention to...."*
- Bold, color coded or boxed type
- Section summaries with simple plain language comments such as *"What does this mean?"*

3. **BALANCE.** Look for validation of information with other everyday experiences that readers are likely to be familiar with. Point out further questions or limitations to the data in a clear fashion for the readers. Remind the audience to compare what the data is "saying" to other sources of information. I/DD personnel may have a tendency to place too much or too little "faith" in data-based findings. Many human service personnel may even attribute unwarranted certainty to numbers, without recognizing the limitations of data and statistics. This bias can often be countered by suggesting to readers that they:

- Ask "why?" if the data is telling them something very different or unexpected
- Remember that data is really only a starting point for more in-depth exploration and analysis. It will often raise more questions than it will answer.

4. **SMALL STEPS.** Caution the audience to "slow down" and avoid jumping to conclusions. Remind readers to not fall victim to an activity trap by immediately seeking "solutions" to perceived issues before exploring the findings in greater detail. Encourage readers to look for trends, convergence of data and repetition of a finding.

5. **BENCHMARKS.** Provide reference points when meaningful benchmarks are available. Appropriately selected benchmarks can provide perspective and help readers to understand how the findings are similar to or differ from comparable data. The use of historical information can also be an informative comparison.

6. **ACTIONABLE.** Supply the reader with prompts about "next steps" and what actions can be considered or further explored based on the more important findings from the analysis. Never assume the audience knows or understands what to do next. If applicable, provide examples of successful actions that others have taken when confronted with similar circumstances and note any major differences. Reference and link resource documents and provide summaries of successful solutions in sidebars in the report to guide thinking and enhance problem-solving.

PUBLISHING REPORTS

THE OPEN PUBLICATION of analytic findings, particularly those related to safety and quality outcomes, is strongly recommended once the organization's leadership has had an opportunity to review and understand what the analysis has found. Publishing reports can help to inform a wider range of stakeholders about important issues that impact the health and safety of the people served by the organization. Publishing results can also send a clear message to the public – and all the stakeholders in the system (including staff, service recipients and their families) - about the importance placed by leadership on open and honest discovery of issues and their prompt correction. It can serve to generate creative ideas about how to make important changes to the service system to enhance quality and reduce risk of harm.

It should be noted that the benefit of such open and public reporting was highlighted in an independent federal evaluation of mortality review conducted by the Government Accountability Office (GAO).[1] After studying a variety of state I/DD system approaches to mortality review and reporting, the GAO concluded that "...*publicly reporting information about mortality review findings helps to ensure transparency in the mortality review process and demonstrates to the public areas where the agency should direct its efforts to improve the quality of care.*"[1]

While it is sometimes viewed as "threatening" by agency leadership and legal personnel at first, public reporting has many benefits that should be promoted and explained to the senior leadership of an I/DD organization. For example, potential benefits that can be achieved through the consistent publication of data and findings include:

- Sharing of information about health and safety issues to a wide audience of stakeholders provides a focus and context for why risk prevention is so important

- It communicates to staff the critical nature of discovery and the value of objective review of issues that may compromise health and safety

- Public reporting demonstrates honesty, openness and transparency

- It strengthens the presence of a culture of safety within your organization

- The analysis and broad communication of findings can help to generate better ideas for quality improvement

- It sends a clear message about the importance leadership places on open and honest reporting

- Consistent analysis and reporting allows the objective tracking of performance against goals

- It provides a basis for illustrating trends and changes in safety, morbidity and mortality

- Public reporting can provide a useful forum for expanding the use of comparative benchmarks and objective measurements of change.

Therefore, open and transparent publication of analytic findings, when done properly, can serve as a robust tool for enhancing risk management and quality improvement in all I/DD service organizations and public systems. It should be strongly encouraged and supported by agency leaders, service recipients and their families, funding entities and actually, all stakeholders in the field of disability services.

PLANNING FOR PUBLICATION

WHEN PLANNING TO WRITE a report or when first designing a publication strategy for sharing data, it is extremely important to clearly identify the purpose of the report/publication, the primary audience for which it is intended, and how it will be communicated. Only then is it possible to appreciate what specific information should be included and what the best format is for communicating the information. In other words, always think carefully about why you want to provide information, to whom it is to be provided and how it will be communicated.

PURPOSE. Just as when planning the roll-out of a new service or support system, it is imperative to understand and clarify the purpose or aim of a data report. This means recognizing why the report is to be published (i.e., what one wants to achieve by sharing the data). To accomplish this, it is necessary to spend time examining how the data analysis can and ultimately will be used by different stakeholders associated with your organization. In other words, effort must be directed toward identifying what kind of information they want and how they can best use it to make decisions. The analysis of data and publication of a report must be focused on purpose. Otherwise, the information that is presented will most likely not be used effectively - or it may even be ignored. Know why the information is being communicated before designing any report.

TARGET AUDIENCE. Who will be reviewing a report is equally important. It should always be clarified before beginning to write the report. There are a wide range of potential users of the information that will be communicated in most data-based reports. Each target audience will most likely need and desire different types of data and prefer different approaches for displaying information. Some will have sophisticated skills and be able to understand more complex and technical data. Others will have limited experience and capacity to understand data. It may therefore be necessary to prepare a variety of presentations and reports that are geared for each audience group. One must carefully think about who will be reviewing the data report and then prepare it (or versions of it) in a manner that can effectively communicate the most important information to each target audience. Factors to consider when examining the potential target audiences include:

- **Internal vs. external reporting.** Are users of the information in the report going to be primarily staff within the organization or is the data going to be shared outside of the agency? A number of legal and public relations issues will need to be addressed for information about a sensitive subject (e.g., accidental or preventable deaths) to be communicated to the public and available to individuals and entities outside of the organization itself. The availability of a data report for general review should not inhibit or prevent publication of sensitive subjects; rather, it may simply mean that the author of the report may need to pay greater attention to wording, context and inclusion of corrective/preventive actions already taken or planned for the near future. It can also be helpful in such instances to provide "plain language" explanations of relevant factors that can be expected to increase risk in the I/DD population (such as higher rates of physical disabilities and co-morbid medical conditions) and to incorporate the use of comparative benchmarks so that the data can be easily referenced to reasonable expectations.

- **Leadership vs. staff.** In large organizations and public I/DD systems that support a large population or cover an extensive geographical area, too much detail can cloud or hide the "big picture" that is often needed by senior leadership so they can quickly grasp important issues, track performance and focus change initiatives on existing and emerging areas of concern. Summary data that highlights the most important findings is usually

91

helpful to leadership. On the other hand, clinical, supervisory and direct support staff may need more specific and detailed data that can help them identify issues and trends for the programs and people they directly support. Technical language should be reserved for users who will be fluent in and familiar with special terms and concepts (e.g., when communicating with health professionals about medical and health data and findings).

- **Service recipients and family members vs. general public.** Data reports about service quality and safety can be an important factor in helping service recipients and their advocates and families make informed decisions about existing or potential service providers. For data to be useful to this audience it must provide program and/or service provider comparisons and be relatively simple to understand. It needs to be focused on issues that have been identified as most important to them. The general public (including oversight entities) may, however, be more interested in systems-based data that reflects broader trends and that can highlight problem areas that may require attention. Knowing the audience and their unique needs is therefore essential for effective communication. The primary audience for any report should influence the level of detail that is provided in the report and the technical nature of the data and its analysis. Different audience groups require different methods for organizing, analyzing and displaying data and associated information. If the preparation of multiple reports is not feasible given allocated resources, begin by reporting data for a select target audience and then, over time, gradually adjust the type and level of information (data) and communication methods that are used in order to meet the needs of the next and different user group. It is also possible to address this issue of variable audience groups by designing a basic and very general report for broad distribution and then supplementing it with more focused and detailed mini-reports or supplements that are geared to more specific target audiences.

METHOD. In the not so distant past, options for publishing data and analytic reports were somewhat limited to cumbersome and expensive print media. Today, digital methods for communicating information are widely available and can be more engaging and adaptable. In fact, methods for sharing data and reports are almost limitless. Your data can now be "published" and communicated to almost every stakeholder audience via methods that are targeted to their interests and needs, including:

- Traditional paper-based reports
- Email summaries with or without attached data files and "mini-reports" or briefs
- Internet sites that have the ability for users to self-select customized information and level of detail geared to their individual interests
- Interactive web-based sites that link to databases and possess the capacity for direct data entry and interaction with the database
- Video and podcasts to present information in a more engaging fashion
- Webinars that include options for interaction with the audience
- Interactive and on-line discussion boards that can allow users to review information and receive instantaneous responses to any questions or other inquiries

- Newsletters, Fact Sheets and "Safety Briefs" that are distributed (electronically or in paper format) on a regular basis can focus on specific findings and highlight special areas of concern.

INFORMATION. Once the primary purpose of a report, the target audience, and preferred method(s) for communicating results have been established it is time to focus on identifying the data and information that should be included in the report. A number of different examples of potential data that can be included are illustrated in the following sections of this chapter. But always remember that the specific data that is included in the report must be dependent upon the topic and aim of the analysis.

> **Important Note:** START SOMEWHERE! It is better to begin organizing, reviewing, analyzing and reporting data findings – even if not perfect – than to do nothing at all because it seems too complicated. Plan and then act. Review and then modify. But, begin to do something with all the data that is being collected and stored. Use the data!

FORMAT REPORTS FOR THE TARGET AUDIENCE

As NOTED EARLIER, it is important to align the format of a report with the needs of the target audience. A few considerations for each of the more common formats used to present I/DD data include:

FORMAL REPORTS. When preparing a large, formal report that includes data-based analytic findings certain strategies can make the report more useful for readers. For instance, always include an *executive summary* of findings that can introduce readers to the structure of and some of the more important findings resulting from the data analysis. Tables of contents, as well as lists of tables and figures with page numbers can also help readers navigate larger reports. Keep in mind that more complex and lengthy reports may not be a very effective communication tool for many potential readers in the field of I/DD. Again, pay careful attention to the needs of the primary audience and the purpose for the communication.

BRIEFS. It can sometimes be more useful to create a series of *briefs* or short reports that focus on specific topics or themes that would normally be contained within a more complex report. Customized briefs can be presented in a way that is easier to digest and understand for most target audiences. Often such briefs are formatted similar to a newsletter where content is presented in shorter and topic-specific sections. Readers can peruse the document and locate topics that are of the most interest to them. Briefs should be written in simple, easy to read language and provide practical information that is geared to the target audience. If it is anticipated that some readers may desire access to more technical information, one can always provide resource links that will not encumber the general reader with highly complex data.

ELECTRONIC PRESENTATIONS. When reviewing findings contained in a larger report, electronic slides are often used to guide your presentation or to illustrate specific data in order to increase awareness and understanding of important facts. The use of presentation slides allows one to 'zoom in' on specific sections of a report in order to highlight findings. However, electronic slides and other material used to emphasize and highlight data do require planning and attention to formatting and design. Each slide should contain a limited amount of information (don't crowd the slide) that is related to a common issue. Slides should be used only as an aid or guide in a presentation and are not intended to be read by the audience. Use slides to illustrate key points and present visual images that can assist the audience to follow the verbal presentation. Avoid including too much detail and narrative. Visual aids should be designed to increase audience interest and engagement, not serve as a substitute for verbal communication.

ACCESSIBILITY IS IMPORTANT. When designing any form of communication, keep in mind that different people may have different abilities and varying needs for accessing and understanding the information. Therefore, it is important to try to create easy to understand summaries, visual presentations and to use a variety of media - in different formats - that can be accessible to many different people. This is especially important in the field of I/DD and for reports that may be read and used by a wider variety of stakeholders, from clinical professionals to service recipients and their families.

Some tips for making a data-based report or presentation as accessible as possible include:

- In written reports and materials, avoid using text that is too small or in colors that provide low contrast with the background (e.g., do not use yellow text on a white page).

- When using images in electronic documents, always be sure to create a brief and succinct text description of the meaning of the image that can be added as a 'tag' for the image. People with low vision who rely on screen readers will have special software "readers" that will read or verbalize the text of these tags. This simple addition can help to ensure all of the content in your report is accessible to people with low vision.

- When possible, create a plain language and/or 'easy read' version of your report. Plain language reports are usually written at a fourth grade reading level referenced to the U.S. education system. (Note: Many electronic word document writing programs allow you to quickly evaluate the reading level of your documents and reports.) Sentences should be succinct, short and only present one concept at a time. The content should be written in an active voice and either avoid technical terms or carefully define words and terms that are complex and not part of the common vernacular. Easy-read versions of reports use multi-media, photographs, clip art, pictures and other visual representations to enhance the meaning of simply written text. Often these illustrations are easier to understand for people with learning disabilities and individuals with I/DD. Illustrated versions should be developed in consultation with the audience of people for which they are being developed, often stakeholder groups. It should be noted that quite often these easy-read versions are also preferred by people without learning disabilities, and are quite effective for communicating more complex findings to individuals who may have limited English fluency or literacy.

Resources: There are a number of resources that can provide more detail about how to better meet accessibility standards and that can help guide the preparation of a data-based report. Two useful guides are listed below:

- **A Guide to Making Easy-Read Information**, prepared by People First New Zealand and published by the New Zealand Office for Disability Issues[2]
- **Am I Making Myself Clear?** published by MENCAP (United Kingdom)[3]

COMMUNICATING DATA EFFECTIVELY

THE PRESENTATION OF DATA that is derived from simple descriptive statistics can be powerful, informative and easy to understand when done correctly. The use of simple data tables and graphical illustrations fall into this category. Tables, charts and graphs can quickly summarize analytical findings while at the same time presenting the detail that some users may desire. A variety of sample tables that can be used to illustrate data commonly reported in the field of I/DD are presented as examples in **Appendix K** (Sample Tables for Presenting Descriptive Statistical Analyses of Typical I/DD Data). Reviewing these examples can provide ideas for how simple descriptive statistics can be effectively displayed and visualized. They can be easily adapted to fit the specific data that most any I/DD organization or large service system wishes to communicate.

A slightly different approach should be used when sharing the findings associated with inferential statistical analysis. When presenting the results of inferential statistics (e.g. a chi-squared test) one should avoid simply presenting numbers, such as the value or probability of the statistic. Absent additional context, such technical information usually fails to convey a clear meaning and is open to gross misinterpretation by naive readers. It is critical to always represent the meaning of the findings through a phrase or sentence. As discussed in previous sections, be sure to provide important contextual information that can affect the interpretation of the result.

For example, an incomplete presentation of data associated with inferential analysis is represented by the following notation:

Change in critical incident rate 2012-2013: chi-square = 4.3, p=0.22

A more useful presentation of the same information would be to more clearly state:

There was a statistically significant increase in the rate of critical incidents reported in 2013 compared to 2012. However, in 2013 the organization also pursued a strategic initiative to improve the compliance in incident reporting. Therefore, the observed increase between 2012 and 2013 may be due, at least in part, to better compliance with reporting rules.

As can be seen, the information presented in the second example is far more informative and less likely to be misinterpreted.

USING GRAPHS TO VISUALIZE DATA

GRAPHS AND CHARTS are helpful tools that can quickly illustrate relationships, trends and patterns that may not be readily apparent when describing data in tables and text. However, graphs and visual figures need to be carefully designed to clearly illustrate and highlight the more important meanings of the data that the author wishes to express. Poorly designed figures can lead to confusion, or worse, to misinterpretation of the information. Visual illustrations and graphs should be designed to be self-explanatory. Nonetheless, it is usually important to include explanatory text when using graphs and figures to ensure that they are correctly interpreted.

CREATING EFFECTIVE GRAPHS AND CHARTS

SOME SIMPLE STRATEGIES that can be used to help select the right type of figure for the illustration of data and guide the design of more effective graphs include:

- Start with a question. Ask *"What message do I want to communicate with this figure?"* Then design the figure/graph to directly answer that question.

- Aim for clear, simple and concise figures that can be interpreted quickly. In most instances, *simple* is more effective than *complex*.

- Consider the amount of data included in the figure and whether it is too little or too much to illustrate the point you are trying to emphasize. Too little information can be just as problematic as too much data.

- Use labels to identify what the data on the graph represents, including the following:
  - Title – what is the graph content all about?
  - Use labels on both axes of a line or bar chart and on all sections of a pie chart
  - Note the source of the data
  - Include a key or legend when using different colors, line styles or shading

Remember to take time to carefully review and evaluate figures before finalizing them. After creating a graph or figure, once again ask whether or not it is clearly able to communicate the desired message. Seek feedback from another individual – ask them to explain what the graph is communicating. Make sure it is easy to understand and that the first thing readers will recognize is the main point that is trying to be expressed. If it is not, ask "why?" Consider whether or not the main message is lost due to too much information or clutter. Think about whether the data is correct and simple to understand. Explore whether or not the vertical and horizontal axes need to be adjusted to more easily illustrate change. Make modifications to the graphs until satisfied that the figure is easy to understand and immediately conveys the message that is intended.

USE DIFFERENT GRAPHS FOR DIFFERENT DATA

THERE ARE MANY varieties of graphs and visual figures than can be used to communicate and illustrate the type of data that is commonly reported in I/DD systems. A few of the more common types of graphs that are most useful when presenting I/DD related data are described and then illustrated below. Take time to select the most appropriate type of graph; experiment with different formats before finalizing and incorporating graphs into a report or presentation. Taking time up front will make a big difference.

DOT PLOTS. Dot plots are relatively simple graphs that are usually very visually appealing and that can clearly illustrate the frequency of different pieces of data contained within a data set. They are most useful for showing categorical data.

When should a dot plot be used?	Dot plots place data values along a common scale. They are best used to compare values across different categories. They tend to be very effective for making relative comparisons because their format takes advantage of strengths of human perception. These plots tend to be less cluttered than other types of figures such as bar charts when presenting data from many different categories.
When should the use of data plots be avoided?	When trying to show change over time.
How can dot plots be made more effective	Order categories by size rather than alphabetically.

The following example of a dot plot shows the number of annual incidents per district for 5 service districts within an agency. Notice that it is easy to see by glancing at the figure that District 1 had the most incidents, followed by District 2. This figure has also added information to the dots about the percent of total incidents represented by each district. This information is optional, and an example of how data labels can add meaning to the figure.

Example of a Dot Plot

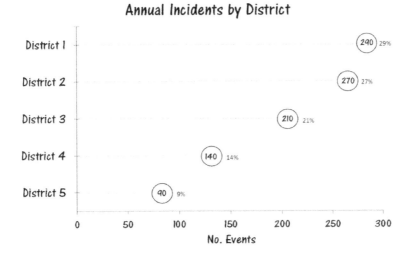

97

PIE CHARTS. This type of graph is frequently used in I/DD reports to illustrate the relative distribution of a variable such as age, type of residential support and/or level/category of disability. Pie charts are usually easy to understand - if constructed correctly.

When should a pie chart be used?	Pie charts are appropriate to use to describe the portions of a categorical data set when the categories represent portions of an entire set of data. For example: a pie chart could be used to illustrate revenue generated by program, where the entire pie chart represents total revenue; or, the number of people by residential setting where the entire pie chart represents all the people served by an organization or system.
When should pie charts be avoided?	Avoid the use of pie charts in the following circumstances: • There are a large number of variables (portions) making the pie chart complicated and cluttered and therefore difficult to interpret • Only a portion of data is being shown, i.e. the pie chart does not represent the whole or 100% of the data related to a variable • There is overlap between categories, e.g., to illustrate the number of people by service line where people receive different types of services from multiple lines • To show change over time (trends)
How can pie charts be made more effective?	Pie charts can be made easier to understand more effective by: • Adding labels to the pie chart that describe both the category and a summary of the 'slice' – such as a percentage or the value that is being represented. [Without this information, it can be more challenging for a reader to discern the relative size of the portions of the pie chart, and therefore, the meaning of the data.] • Avoiding the use of 3-D presentations since they can make it visually more difficult to discern the relative size of the 'pie slices,' sometimes resulting in a distorted representation of your data.

The example of a pie chart on the next page illustrates the percent of a service population by districts within an I/DD organization. A pie chart is appropriate for this type of data since the chart represents the entire population and there is no overlap between districts. Data labels with the percentage of the population for each district have been added. Note that without these labels, it could be challenging to discern whether District 5 is the same size or smaller than District 4. Pie charts such as this are relatively easy to construct in most spreadsheet programs, although attention must be given to how you first layout your data table used to construct the graph.

Example of a Pie Chart

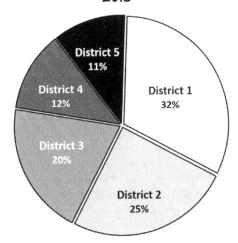

BAR GRAPHS. Bar graphs are often the most common method for illustrating data in I/DD reports. When prepared correctly they are visually appealing and easy to understand for the average reader. As an example, the following bar graph illustrates the number of people employed by an I/DD program across four years. A quick review of this chart allows the reader to see a perceptible trend: the presence of a consistent but small increase in employment across the time period.

Example of a Bar Graph

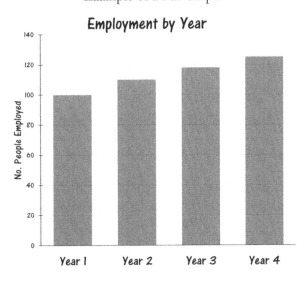

When incorporating bar graphs into a report consider the following;

When should a bar graph be used?	Bar graphs are frequently used to compare data across groups or categories. They can also be used to compare change over time. This type of graph can be used to show an entire set of data, or to show select groups or categories (in contrast to pie charts). Bar charts are useful for quickly illustrating comparisons between groups.
When should bar graphs be avoided?	Do not use a bar graph: • When illustrating small changes over time. Small changes are hard to visually recognize in bar graphs, especially when you are not able to condense the Y (vertical) axis. In these instances you should consider the use of a line graph. • For more complicated data sets that contain more than 3 variables. Many types of graphs will tend to appear cluttered and difficult to interpret when too much data is included. It is better to use multiple graphs, each with smaller data sets to make it easier for your reader to interpret the information. If you do use more than one graph in this way, make sure your Y-axis is consistent across graphs.
How can bar graphs be made more effective?	To make it easier to read your bar graph try using data labels to clarify the meaning of the data Keep it simple. Visually simple and uncluttered graphs can be quickly and easily understood. Complex graphs are easily misinterpreted or ignored. Do not use a stacked bar graph with many different levels since they can be extremely difficult to understand.

LINE GRAPHS. A good way to illustrate changes that take place across time periods is with the use of a line graph. When using this type of chart to visually illustrate data it is important to think about the following:

When should a line graph be used?	Line graphs are useful for displaying changes over time. They tend to be better than bar graphs at showing small changes, and are also more effective at illustrating change in multiple groups over the same time period.
When should line graphs be avoided?	Line graphs can become confusing when showing change for a large number of groups or when the differences between groups are extremely small and lines overlap.
How can line graphs be made more effective?	Advise the audience to exercise caution and not to over-interpret a potential change illustrated in a line graph. In I/DD services some change can be expected over time due to chance or natural fluctuation. Consider using methods such as statistical testing to assess whether observed changes are real and of sufficient magnitude to warrant further attention or are probably due to chance.

In the following example, a line graph illustrates the number of people employed by two different programs across four years. In contrast to the earlier data shown in the bar graph, this chart adds another level of detail (program) that shows an inconsistent pattern in employment in the two programs. The line connecting the data over time makes it easy to see that that the number of people employed has increased in Program 1 and actually decreased over time in Program 2.

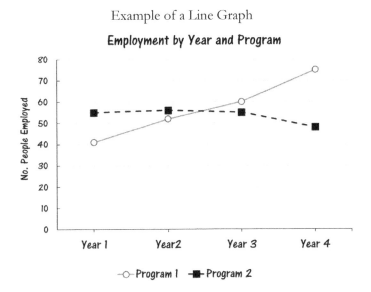

Example of a Line Graph

AVOID TOO MUCH DATA IN GRAPHS

THERE ARE A NUMBER of design flaws that should be avoided when constructing graphs. Some of the more important of these are presented below along with some strategies that can be used to improve the use of figures and graphs.

AVOID EXCESS DATA. Do not include too much information in a graph or figure. Excess data and information can cause the main message to become lost in the clutter. Use graphs to visually illustrate and highlight major points and differences; do not force a reader to search for the meaning and message. Make it "jump out" and be immediately recognized.

In the next example, the pie chart is intended to show differences in the percentage of incidents that have taken place by program location over the course of one month. However, given the presence of 25 separate locations, there is far too much information on the graph to make it useful. For instance, it is difficult to visually discern any pattern and next to impossible to compare the relative size or proportion of incidents that occurred within each location. There is simply too much information presented on this one graph to serve any useful purpose. It is poorly designed and used inappropriately.

Example of an Ineffective Display of Data

Incidents by Location

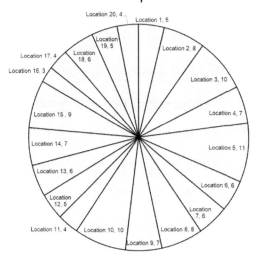

A more effective approach would be to present the data regarding locations in a table and then consolidate the data by combining program locations into districts, illustrating the latter using a pie chart. An example is shown below.

Example of an Effective Display of Data

Incidents by District & Program Location

Program Location	District	No. Incidents	Percent of Total Incidents
Location 1	1	5	
Location 2		8	
Location 3		10	
Location 4		7	
Location 5		11	
District 1 Total		41	31%
Location 6	2	6	
Location 7		6	
Location 8		8	
Location 9		7	
Location 10		10	
District 2 Total		37	28%
Location 11	3	4	
Location 12		5	
Location 13		6	
Location 14		7	
Location 15		9	
District 3 Total		31	24%
Location 16		3	
Location 17		4	
Location 18		6	
Location 19		5	
Location 20		4	
District 4 Total		22	17%
TOTAL INCIDENTS		131	100%

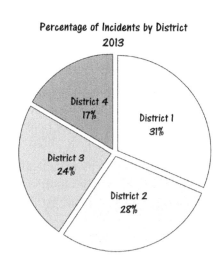

When the percent of incidents by district is shown along with data labels on the pie chart, and is supplemented with more specific and well organized data in a table, it is much easier to see the differences in the number and percentage of incidents across the four districts. If desired, pie charts for each district could also be illustrated to show the differences by location within each district.

USE THE CORRECT SCALE. Avoid over-emphasizing differences by using a small scale. This type of data manipulation can be very confusing and even misleading. While using a beginning point of zero on the Y-axis may seem appropriate, it can disguise or hide meaningful change in certain instances; in contrast compressing the scale can exaggerate small differences and suggest a significant difference or change when there really is not one. For example, the first bar graph illustrated below uses a full scale that suggests there has been very small growth in employment across the four years. The second chart presents the same data but does not begin with zero on the vertical (Y) axis. It therefore increases the perception of relative difference between years. Use abbreviated scales with caution and only to emphasize a difference when this represents the "message" you are trying to convey. If the scale is adjusted or different throughout a report, make sure this is clearly noted in order to avoid misinterpretation of the data (and possible claims of intentional deception).

Two Examples of Employment Data Using Different Scales

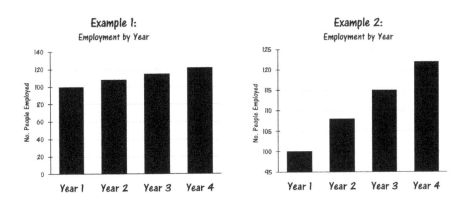

When deciding what y-axis scale should be used, remember to:

- Check the automatic scaling feature of the spreadsheet program to make sure it constructs the graph appropriately and incorporates the correct and intended scale;
- Be consistent throughout your report and clearly identify any deviations from scaling that is the most frequently used in the report or presentation;
- Try to use the same amount of distance across the axes to represent similar amounts of change;

- Have a maximum value that is large enough to incorporate all of your data (always check the default scaling values to make sure they are appropriate);
- Have a maximum value that is small enough to use most of the graph space for the display of your data (i.e., do not leave a lot of blank area on the top of the graph's vertical axis);
- Consider using a base value of zero when possible and appropriate. While it is not always necessary to begin a scale with zero, starting with a different value can be misleading to the audience unless it is clearly noted in the report or presentation;
- Use units that are small enough to add meaning but not so small that they clutter the graph and make it difficult to read.

BEWARE OF SHORT-TERM CHANGES. Don't jump to conclusions and highlight changes that take place over very short time periods. Instead look carefully at larger patterns across and within the data. Be especially careful in graphing changes over very short time periods as the amount of change that is visually depicted can be easily misinterpreted. Before presenting such change, consider using other methods such as statistical testing to make sure observed differences are substantial enough to be highlighted in a graph.

The example below shows how easily a faulty conclusion could be drawn from a graphical display of short-term change. In this example, data are illustrated regarding the rate of hospital visits per 1000 people served by an I/DD agency. Viewing this graph without looking more carefully at the data itself could easily suggest that the number of hospital visits is increasing rather dramatically. However, by viewing a longer time period for the same data set, it becomes evident that the rate of hospital visits has a tendency to fluctuate a great deal by month. One can also see that the three month time period illustrated in the first graph actually appears to be within the normal fluctuation limits for the rate of hospital visits. Only displaying data for the shorter 3-month time period was misleading and suggested that hospital visits were rising very quickly.

Two Examples of Hospital Visits Using Short and Longer Term Time Periods

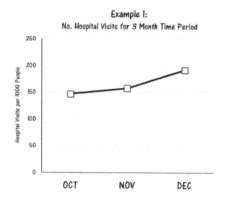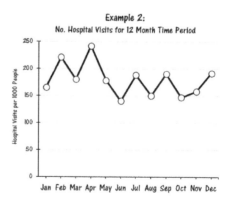

DO NOT OVERUSE GRAPHS AND FIGURES

FOR SMALL DATA SETS, a simple table is often the best method for presenting data. Use the presentation method that presents the data most clearly and in a format where it is easiest to discern its meaning and the primary message that one wants to communicate. Do not use graphs when the data does not show any meaningful differences or change. In these instances it is usually best to present the information in a simple table or chart or even in narrative format. Graphs should be used strategically to highlight important points. Overuse leads to clutter, redundancy and distraction in a report or presentation,

USING DATA TO MITIGATE RISK

IN ORDER TO EFFECTIVELY manage risk, it is important to identify and measure actual and potential risk factors and events on an ongoing basis. Measurement can provide important information about the potential severity of the risk, the scope of its potential impact, and the resources that are necessary to mitigate and prevent it. In turn, the information obtained from measurement can be used to select and prioritize the most effective response to adverse events. Data is needed to measure most factors impacting safety and risk. Use it. And use it effectively!

DATA AND THE QUALITY FRAMEWORK

THE CMS QUALITY FRAMEWORK was presented in an earlier chapter and is particularly relevant to a discussion regarding the use of data and the results from data analysis to manage risk of harm and improve the quality of services and supports. Information obtained from data systems can be an extremely important tool for designing effective quality systems and risk mitigation interventions. It can be very useful for discovering important areas that need to be addressed, providing guidance on how issues can be best resolved and for helping measure and evaluate the effectiveness of improvement initiatives. The four functions embedded within the framework and their relationship to data are described below.

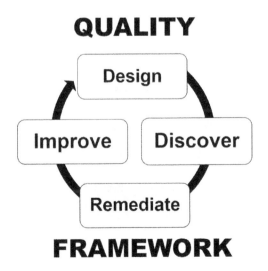

DESIGN. The use of objective data about the safety, quality and the performance of a service system can be used to guide planning regarding which methods are most appropriate for the discovery of issues and the remediation and monitoring of their ongoing status and improvement. When in the process of redesigning or modifying a quality assurance and improvement system, historic data can be very useful as a means of informing the design process so it can more effectively ensure risk mitigation and service quality. A reliance solely on monitoring to discover problems tends to drive a reactive environment where personnel in a service organization are continually responding to events that have already happened. Instead, it is usually more effective to reduce or eliminate systemic factors (the "why" bad things happen) and focus on prevention. This approach can have a much more positive impact on reducing harm and enhancing quality.

An organization should periodically review where information about its performance is lacking but could be of enormous help in creating positive change. A few examples of some methods for using data and analytic tools to design and modify systems include the use of:

- **Structured planning tools** that can help organize the information that is available about internal and external factors that affect an organization's performance and that can provide guidance that is actionable. In this regard, one should consider a basic method such as the Strengths, Weaknesses, Opportunities, and Threats (SWOT) analysis.[4] While originally designed for use in a for-profit environment, the SWOT approach can be useful in the not-for-profit sector, including in I/DD organizations.

- **Failure Mode and Effect Analysis (FMEA)** can be a useful tool for examining where and how processes can fail before they are implemented. Weaknesses in a planned process that have a high probability of occurrence or could result in a very severe event can be corrected before an adverse event takes place.

- **Learning from historical patterns and past occurrences.** Data is very useful as a way to identify patterns of risk by examining past events, trends and the relationships between different variables. Efforts can be directed toward designing systems to more quickly recognize patterns and identify risk factors so they can be corrected in a more timely and effective fashion.

DISCOVER. Objective data that is supported by analytic processes can help answer "who," "what," "when" and "where" questions that can aid in the discovery of events that require closer examination. Data can be used to identify both successes and failures within a system. Such data can be derived from processes that have been established to monitor certain events or outcomes (such as incident reporting). The data can be structured to signal changes in expected patterns, allowing more timely intervention. As noted previously, it is important to always look for areas of convergence across multiple sources of data to identify common traits or issues that appear to impact a number of different people or multiple service settings.

Consider the following examples that represent ways to inform the discovery of risk by looking for patterns and trends related to:

- Lack of change in health status or behavior where change had been anticipated;

106

- Local program or geographic areas exhibiting little positive growth or very slow change;

- Extremes – relatively high rate of poor outcomes or extremely low rates of poor outcomes that may suggest reporting compliance issues;

- High severity of sentinel events, presence of 'never' events; costly patterns; "near misses" (i.e., incidents where sentinel events are narrowly avoided);

- Systemic failures identified in case reviews – such as incident or mortality reviews, identification of systemic factors that resulted in poor decisions, delayed help seeking;

- Clusters of potentially preventable events, the presence of multiple instances of urgent care for normally non-urgent issues (e.g., hospitalizations for chronic conditions such as diabetes or asthma may indicate subpar management – or hospitalization for UTIs that can normally be treated at a doctor's office); and/or

- Individual risk profiles that allow proactive identification of people who fit identified patterns of health and behavioral risks that have been identified in other service recipients.

REMEDIATE. Analytic processes can often help answer "why" questions and aid in the identification of important systemic issues that are contributing to events (both good and bad). The use of appropriate analytic methods, often initiated by the review of data and findings from data analysis, can also help to target remedial actions that can directly result in effective risk mitigation and quality improvement changes to a service system.

Methods such as Root Cause Analysis (RCA), Apparent Cause Analysis (ACA), structured debriefing, and incident review can and should be used to supplement data analysis to enhance an organization's remediation activities. In addition, I/DD organizations should consider the active involvement of stakeholders that can help make remediation efforts far more effective and responsive to the issues and concerns of those most directly affected by risk mitigation and quality improvement activities. Service recipients, line staff and many others (e.g., advocates, family members, community employers) possess varied and valuable perspectives that can help translate information that can be used to implement practical approaches for the correction of risk factors that compromise the safety and quality of supports. Sharing data findings with such stakeholders and openly discussing the "real" causes of adverse events and problems with service quality will usually lead to faster and more direct remediation. Therefore, organizations should always make an effort to ask those closest to the issue "why" things happen once data analysis signals the need for closer examination of issues.

IMPROVE. Objective data can be extremely useful in assessing the effectiveness of remediation and quality improvement initiatives. It can help determine whether or not change strategies and improvement activities are actually resulting in the desired change. Such performance or outcome measurement is an essential component of an effective quality improvement process.

The effective use of objective information requires organizations to consistently engage in structured activities that can collect and integrate your data, and can be used to target corrective and preventive actions based on the findings from your analysis. The use of data is effective when it forms the basis for open communication designed to educate and promote positive change, and, when it is used to evaluate the effectiveness of change efforts. Data-based assessment and management are an essential aspect of any organization's safety and quality improvement system.

INTEGRATE DATA AND FINDINGS

PAY SPECIAL ATTENTION to how findings from the analysis of data are integrated and synthesized across topics and program units within the entire organization or service system. Such integration of information helps to develop a more complete understanding of what factors are most likely exerting the greatest influence on safety, quality and organizational outcomes. "Findings" that are based on a very limited set of data, particularly when from a small sample or biased collection method, will have inherent flaws that can only lead to faulty conclusions and ineffective "solutions." This not only wastes valuable time and resources, but also erodes faith in the usefulness of the data that is being reported throughout the organization. Therefore, analytic processes should always strive to achieve both vertical and horizontal integration of information.

- **Vertical integration** of data is critical – integration of information across the three basic levels of the organization/system, starting with the individual, moving to the program (particular setting, provider, unit, area, region, etc.) and finally across the service system as a whole (i.e., organization, state I/DD system, inter-state provider programs, etc.). Vertical integration also requires active communication and actual use of the findings and data by the different levels within an organizational hierarchy. Individuals, families, agency leadership, management, direct support, clinicians – all aspects of the organization should be able to see and potentially use the information. Delivering this information in formats that are targeted to the specific interests and needs of the different audiences will assist people to use the information in a more effective fashion.

- **Horizontal integration** and cross-analysis of data is equally important. Organizations should strive to review and incorporate information across multiple data sets, information sources, and variables. For instance, horizontal integration seeks to promote understanding by combining and analyzing data from reporting systems related to unusual incidents, injuries, restraint utilization, abuse and neglect reporting, adverse drug events/medication error reporting, licensing and certification, complaint reports, etc. Using such multiple data sources can help to confirm findings, and more clearly identify factors that may be driving a particular finding.

This concept of vertical and horizontal integration is illustrated in the diagram on the next page. To most effectively use this approach, it is extremely important to carefully look for emerging themes, analyze the inter-relationships of variables and cross validate any emerging hypotheses and conclusions that result from the analysis of data. Ask questions such as *"Does the issue or concern appear in more than one data system or program site?" "Is there any relationship between this variable and another one, and if so, what is it and why might it be present?"* Exploring issues such as these can lead to more effective focus on the most important issues. It usually requires additional analysis that can identify "modifiable determinants," i.e., factors that can be changed or acted upon. That in turn can guide the development of truly effective interventions that reduce risk and lead to successful quality improvement initiatives.

An Integrated Approach for Improving Safety and Quality

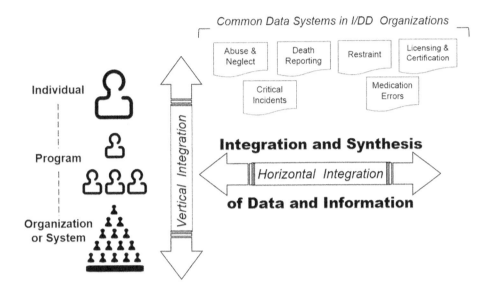

Take the time to synthesize and integrate data to create a truly comprehensive approach to risk management and quality improvement. The data is always there – do something positive with it!

Note: The on-line course *Using Data as a Quality Tool in DD* contains a number of optional learning modules that incorporate step-by-step video demonstrations designed to enhance the learning experience and that include:

- How to Organize Data in a Spreadsheet or Database

- How to Calculate a Standard Deviation

- How to Calculate Student's t-Test

- How to Calculate an Age-adjusted Rate

As in all of the internet based courses in the series, also included in the on-line course is a module on *System Design in Developmental Disabilities*. Note that the material associated with this comprehensive module is also available in print as a Supplement to the book series. See the **udiscovering** internet site for details regarding both the printed books and access to the on-line courses.

To learn more about the *Risk Management in DD* series of on-line courses interested readers are encouraged to review resources available at:

http://www.udiscovering.org

REFERENCES

CHAPTER 2

[1] Reason J. (1998). *Human error.* New York: Cambridge University Press.

[2] Reason J. (1998). Achieving a safe culture: theory and practice. *Work and Stress,* 12(3), p. 294.

[3] Marx D. (2007). *Patient safety and "just culture."* Outcome Engineering. Presentation accessed April 1, 2015 at: http://www.health.ny.gov/professionals/patients/patient_safety/conference/2007/docs/patient safety_ and_the_just_culture.pdf

[4] Leape L. & Berwick D.M. (2005). Five years after "To Err is Human": What have we learned? *Journal of the American Medical Association,* 293(19), 2384-2390.

[5] Norman D. (2002). *The design of everyday things, First Edition.* New York: Basic Books.

[6] Spath P. (2000). *Error Reduction in Health Care: A Systems Approach to Improving Patient Safety.* San Francisco: Jossey-Bass.

[7] Botwinick L., Bisognano M., & Haraden C. (2006). *Leadership guide to patient safety.* IHI Innovation Series. Institute for Healthcare Improvement. Available at: https://www.IHI.org

CHAPTER 3

[1] Gates B. (2013). My Plan to Fix the World's Biggest Problems. *The Wall Street Journal.* January 26-27, 2013, C1.

[2] CMS. (2002). U.S. Department of Health and Human Services, Center for Medicare and Medicaid Services. *Letter to State Medicaid Directors,* dated August 29, 2002.

CHAPTER 4

[1] Ovide S. (2013). Big data, big blunders: Five big mistakes and how companies avoid them. *Wall Street Journal. March 11, 2013,* R4.

CHAPTER 8

[1] Nickerson S., Perkins D. & Smith E. (1985). *The Teaching of Thinking.* Hillsdale, NJ: Lawrence Relbaum Associated.

[2] Gordis L. (1996*). Epidemiology.* Philadelphia: WB Saunders.

[3] NCI. (2013). *National Core Indicators.* Human Services Research Institute (HSRI) and the National Association of State Directors of Developmental Disabilities Services (NASDDDS). Available at: http://www.nationalcoreindicators.org.

[4]The Henry J Kaiser Family Foundation. (2013). *State Health Facts*. Available at: http://kff.org/statedata/

[5]U.S. Department of Health and Human Services. (2013). *Healthy People 2020*. Available at: http://www.healthypeople.gov/

[6]2003-2008 Influenza Activity in Massachusetts, Massachusetts Department of Public Health. Available at: http://www.mass.gov/eohhs/

CHAPTER 9

[1] U.S. Government Accountability Office (2008). *Medicaid home and community-based waivers: CMS should encourage states to conduct mortality reviews for individuals with developmental disabilities*. Report to the Ranking Member, U.S. Committee on Finance, U.S. Senate. (GAO-08-529).

[2]Office for Disability Issues. (2013). *Guide for Making Easy Read Information*. People First New Zealand, New Zealand Office for Disability Issues. Available at: http://www.odi.govt.nz/resources/guides-and-toolkits/disability-perspective/resources/plain-language.html.

[3]MENCAP. (2002). *Am I Making Myself Clear? Mencap's guidelines for accessible writing*. MENCAP, United Kingdom. Available at: http://www.easy-read-online.co.uk/media/10609/making-myself-clear.pdf.

[4]Quincy R., Shuang Lu, and Chien-Chung Huang. (2012). *SWOT Analysis: Raising Capacity of Your Organization*. Huamin Research Center, School of Social Work, Rutgers University. Available at: http://socialwork.rutgers.edu/Libraries/Huamin/Brochure_2.sflb.

APPENDICES

Appendix A

How Strong is Your Organization's Culture of Safety?

Effective and meaningful risk management requires the presence of an organizational culture of safety and a "readiness" to consistently use structured and analytic tools to identify problems and take action to prevent future adverse events.

Carefully review the following statements to assess your organization's readiness to implement a truly comprehensive approach to risk management and its culture of safety. Check those characteristics that apply to your organization now. Think about how you can address "**obstacles**" or "**barriers**" to establishing a meaningful culture of safety that you have identified. Laying the proper "groundwork" will help make your efforts to promote safety and mitigate risk of harm within your organization much easier and more effective.

☐ Leadership tends to avoid the active identification of problems that may compromise safety and waits until something bad happens before acting.

☐ When an adverse event does take place leadership usually "points the finger" and tries to blame staff for making a mistake.

☐ It is unusual for my organization to analyze and use data about adverse incidents to target areas for risk mitigation.

☐ Managers and supervisors within my organization rarely focus on trying to understand <u>why</u> a problem has taken place, especially when the reason may be faulty management decisions or poorly designed organizational systems.

☐ Leadership and managers/supervisors typically do not communicate with front line staff and make decisions about safety in isolation (i.e., without the active involvement of staff).

☐ Managers and supervisors do not actively seek out feedback from staff and consumers concerning what they can do to improve safety and quality within the organization.

☐ There are very few or no formal written policies and guidelines regarding the use of risk management tools such as risk screening, root cause analysis, mortality review, incident reporting and/or failure mode and effects analysis. What policies exist, are not widely understood nor used on a regular basis by staff within the organization.

☐ Our organizational "culture" (its traditional way of responding to incidents) usually focuses on minimizing exposure to negative criticism or potential litigation.

☐ In general, there is not very much teamwork within my work unit or organization.

☐ My organization does not have a formal and written safety plan.

☐ There is no risk management policy or entity (e.g., staff, committee) assigned to focus on the reduction of risk and improvement of safety within my organization.

☐ Leadership within my organization seems to be more concerned with covering up or hiding problems rather than finding or fixing them.

☐ My organization typically does not focus on preventing harm to people but rather emphasizes punishing those who may be responsible for the harm.

☐ When someone is hurt or suffers from an "avoidable" death my organization usually goes for a "quick fix" that does not really correct any systemic issues or problems.

☐ Most staff would agree that our organization does not try to learn from mistakes and errors.

☐ Most staff are afraid they will be disciplined if they make a mistake or report that an adverse event almost took place in their workplace.

☐ When something "bad" happens, my organization tries to find a solution only by talking with people within the agency and does not usually seek information from outside sources (e.g., other agencies, other industries) on possible corrective and preventive strategies.

☐ Professional and clinical staff do not pay attention to or seek out input from direct support staff when it comes to designing programs or identifying risks.

☐ My organization does not have a culture that seeks constant improvement, but rather only implements change when it is forced to.

☐ My organization does not share or publish the results of data analyses and aggregate analytic reviews (i.e., share findings and results from mortality and incident reporting with staff, service recipients and the public at large).

☐ OTHER Barrier:

Number of Obstacles/Barriers: _____

READINESS PLAN: Summarize the top 3 barriers that may be interfering with establishing a true culture of safety within your organization. Note how these could be effectively addressed, who would be best to work on the change and how you would know when the issue was resolved.

Obstacle 1:

_____

How it will be addressed:

_____
_____

Who will do it: _____ Timeline: _____

Readiness Indicator(s):

_____
_____

Obstacle 2:

_____

How it will be addressed:

_____
_____

Who will do it: _____ Timeline: _____

Readiness Indicator(s):

_____
_____

Obstacle 3:

_____

How it will be addressed:

_____
_____

Who will do it: _____ Timeline: _____

Readiness Indicator(s):

_____
_____

APPENDIX B

Data Analysis in Developmental Disabilities
CHECKLIST FOR ASSESSING YOUR DATA SYSTEM

In order for any analysis of information and data to be valid and useful to your organization it should meet certain basic standards. Some basic criteria you can use to evaluate the data you use in your organization are listed in the checklist below. Carefully review these factors to assess the readiness of your organization's data for use in efforts to mitigate risk and enhance quality of services. Check those characteristics that apply to your data now. Note special issues, concerns and problems that exist in your data systems for each of the standards. Identify how you can address "problems" or the absence of particular criteria so that your data can be better used for identifying important issues that affect the health and safety of the people you serve and for guiding improvement initiatives within your organization. List activities that can form the basis of an improvement plan that can help make your data more valid and useful over time.

Check (✓) Further Review Needed	STANDARD Description of Data Requirements	NOTES Major Issues and Concerns
☐	**RELIABLE.** Information and data used in your system are accurate and consistent across settings, programs and reporters. ☐ Standard report forms and/or the same electronic methods are used by all reporters for mandated information reporting ☐ Operational definitions have been established for describing variables for data that is required and must be reported ☐ Report forms or electronic report systems use pre-established codes and check-off categories for collecting essential information and limit narrative recording ☐ Report forms and electronic data collection methods are complete and include all required information (i.e., all essential fields are consistently filled in). ☐ Periodic probes are conducted to assess the accuracy of information that is included on the report form ☐ Probes are conducted to assess compliance with regulatory and/or policy requirements for reporting, both through internal systems and for compliance with external reporting requirements ☐ Designated persons are identified who complete, review, and receive data report forms ☐ Designated reporters have received the same training and have access to written or electronic guides available to assure consistency of responses on forms ☐ Specific time-lines are established for reporting incidents and other required events ☐ Information from different sources is compared for all or a random sample of cases to check accuracy and reliability ☐ When report forms are forwarded off-site for data entry, the data is reviewed and corrected before it is entered into a database ☐ Other activities that increase reliability:	

Check (✓) Further Review Needed	**STANDARD** Description of Data Requirements	**NOTES** Major Issues and Concerns
☐	**VALID.** Information and data used by your organization are useful and can answer important questions concerning the issue under study as evidenced by: ☐There is sufficient data and sample size is large enough to draw conclusions when data is analyzed ☐The data uses recognized codes for classifying events when the data analysis will incorporate external benchmarks (e.g., ICD coding) ☐Information about client and service/program characteristics important to the issue under study is immediately available or directly included in the database ☐Information about services and supports important to the issue under study is available or directly included in the database ☐Data is reviewed and corrections are made before it is analyzed ☐Data is corrected or updated when new information becomes available (e.g., following investigations, identification of coding errors) ☐Technical (e.g., clinical) information is reviewed by a professional familiar with the issue under study to assure its relevance and validity ☐Other activities or factors that increase validity of your data:	

☐	**COMPREHENSIVE.** Data is collected on all persons served by the organization for events and incidents that are being studied. Screening takes place to identify those incidents or data points that may require more detailed review. All or most of the factors that are considered important for understanding and analyzing your organization's desired outcomes are included in the data report or integrated database, as follows:
	
	☐ Data includes all persons actively served by the organization including:
	
	    ○ Persons receiving residential services and supports
	
	    ○ Persons receiving in-home and person-centered/controlled supports or funding
	
	    ○ Persons receiving vocational or day services or supports or funding	

Check (✓) Further Review Needed	STANDARD Description of Data Requirements	NOTES Major Issues and Concerns

	○ Persons receiving service coordination or funding by the organization for coordination of services
	
	○ Persons receiving any other direct or indirect service, support or funding provided by the organization
	
	☐ Incident data includes persons who have been served by the organization within the past 3 to 4 months but who may be either permanently or temporarily served by another organization, including:
	
	  ○ Persons in hospitals or other acute or sub-acute care facilities
	
	  ○ Persons in nursing homes or other long-term care facilities
	
	  ○ Persons in residential schools or other similar settings
	
	  ○ Persons in prisons or other criminal justice facilities
	
	☐ Event or Incident Data includes
	
	  ○ Age and gender
	  ○ Location and time of incident
	  ○ Party responsible for health and welfare at time of incident (if not self)
	  ○ Type of incident (see recording requirements for unusual incidents)
	  ○ Events that were related to the reported unusual incidents, such as:
	    ▪ Restraint
	    ▪ Abuse/neglect allegation
	    ▪ Assaults
	    ▪ Injuries
	    ▪ Need for 911 intervention
	    ▪ Emergency interventions (e.g., for choking)
	  ○ Linkages to data that can provide information regarding:
	    ▪ Medication use and history
	    ▪ Diagnoses (medical)
	    ▪ Disability (type and level)
	    ▪ Mobility and communication status
	    ▪ Major services, as applicable
	      ● Residential supports
	      ● Vocational/day supports
	      ● Family supports
	      ● Behavioral supports
	      ● Other clinical services
	    ▪ Primary medical care provider	

Check (✓) Further Review Needed	STANDARD Description of Data Requirements	NOTES Major Issues and Concerns
	○ Other:	

☐	**USEFUL.** Data provides information that is understandable to managers, clinicians, quality/risk personnel and agency leadership. The information that is provided is organized and actionable and is used to make change in practices.
	
	☐ Data is analyzed using accepted standards of statistical analysis
	
	☐ Data is risk adjusted, where possible
	
	☐ Data is reviewed and used by personnel on a consistent and regular basis
	
	☐ Data is presented in regular reports that can be used to identify historical, current and emerging trends that require additional analysis or review
	
	☐ Data is aggregated on a regular basis to provide information on patterns and trends associated with:
	
	    ○ Causes
	    ○ Locations
	    ○ Individual characteristics related to high incidence of incidents
	
	☐ Used by agency staff to make decisions and establish improvement targets
	
	☐ Data that indicates a need for corrective or preventative intervention leads to prompt notification of designated persons, as applicable
	
	☐ Data includes comparative benchmarks to provide context and to allow determination of unusual events, patterns or trends
	
	☐ Other actions that increase the usefulness of your data:	

☐	**CONFIDENTIAL & ACCESSIBLE.** Data meets all applicable confidentiality and privacy requirements and is available to the people who use it. Information and data can be accessed in a variety of formats. ☐ Personal data meets legal requirements for privacy and does not disclose	

Check (✓) Further Review Needed	STANDARD Description of Data Requirements	NOTES Major Issues and Concerns
	unrelated sensitive information	

	☐ Individual incident data is easily accessed by persons who will need it to review and follow-up on the incident, including:
	
	   ○ Case managers, service coordinators
	   ○ Designated quality assurance personnel
	   ○ Designated clinicians (e.g., nursing staff)
	   ○ Program managers
	   ○ Public agency personnel responsible for oversight	

	☐ Group (population) data that is aggregated is readily accessible by persons who are responsible for overseeing services, establishing quality and improvement targets and managing providers and support systems:
	
	   ○ Public agency leadership
	   ○ Public agency managers and quality assurance persons
	   ○ quality assurance personnel
	   ○ Provider agency leadership
	   ○ Program managers (as applicable)	

	☐ Regular reports (e.g., annual) are available for public review and are organized and presented in easy to read formats	
	☐ Other actions that increase the accessibility of your data:	
☐	**TIMELY.** Data is current and can be used to guide decisions.	
	☐ Data reflects all events for the report/analysis time period	
	☐ Data is not used only for historical reporting, but is current and reflects existing conditions	
	☐ Data is always submitted by reporters following an incident within a designated time period that is not longer than 1 week	
	☐ Aggregate data is analyzed on a regular basis to promote quality improvement	

Check (✓) Further Review Needed	STANDARD Description of Data Requirements	NOTES Major Issues and Concerns
	initiatives that are responsive to current issues. ☐ Other actions that increase the timeliness of your data:	
☐	**PARSIMONIOUS.** Data is not duplicative and is not confusing. ☐ Duplicative data fields or reports are reconciled and consolidated when appropriate ☐ Data definitions are reviewed on a regular basis to guide clarification and consolidation activities ☐ Data fields that are not used for analysis or reporting are eliminated (streamlined) ☐ Review takes place on a regular basis to identify where more than one data field is being used for the same construct or variable – the similar data is retained and the more complicated data is eliminated ☐ Other actions that reduce duplication of data:	

☐	**INTEGRATED.** Data is linked to related information and allows easy analysis of the relationship to other related variables that are captured within the organization's information management systems so that a more holistic picture can be generated of performance, quality and risk/safety.
	
	☐ Stovepipe (separate) data systems have easy-to-configure linkages to incident data
	    ○ Demographic data
	    ○ Medical records data
	    ○ Medication data and Medication administration error data
	    ○ Behavior management and restraint data
	    ○ Program and planning data (e.g., residential, vocational, educational,	

Check (✓) Further Review Needed	STANDARD Description of Data Requirements	NOTES Major Issues and Concerns
	support plan, risk screening)	
	☐ Injury, abuse/neglect and unusual incident data is easily linked to data (by person, program, provider, demographic and service variables)	
	☐ Patterns of related variables are consistently identified and used by leadership to target areas for quality improvement	
	☐ Vertical integration is present, i.e., data can be easily combined from the individual to the program to the system levels	
	☐ Horizontal integration is present, i.e., data for individual settings or programs can be combined and analyzed based on the type of setting or program	
	☐ Cross-variable analysis is used on a regular basis and included in reports and improvement planning	
	☐ Data is used to inform the system's quality assurance and quality improvement efforts	
	☐ Other actions to increase the integration of your data:	
☐	**ORGANIZED & ANALYZED.** Data is organized to facilitate understanding and analysis. The analysis of data is performed by qualified persons on a regular basis to identify issues and trends.	
	☐ Data is categorized into useful groups by variable	
	☐ Large data sets can be collapsed into meaningful groupings	
	☐ Data can be simply aggregated into a format for electronic analysis and development of graphs and charts	
	☐ Aggregate data is provided in easy to read tables, charts and/or graphs	
	☐ Personnel or consultants who analyze data have specialized knowledge regarding appropriate statistical analysis issues that impact the topic	
	☐ Analysis is conducted regularly to show trends over time for programs, providers, service areas/regions and the system	
	☐ Analysis is conducted regularly to show patterns and inter-relationships of variables for individuals, programs, providers, areas/regions and the system	

Check (✓) Further Review Needed	STANDARD Description of Data Requirements	NOTES Major Issues and Concerns
	☐ Basic descriptive statistics are used to illustrate trends and patterns	
	☐ Rates (number per population unit) are used to compare incidents across groups or systems	
	☐ Where useful and valid, inferential statistics are used to identify significant differences over time and between groups	
	☐ Where possible, data is risk adjusted using accepted statistical procedures	
	☐ Comparative benchmarks are used appropriately to reference data and identify differences of concern	
	☐ Other actions that increase the organization and analysis of data:	

☐	**COMMUNICATED.** Data summaries and reports are issued on a regular basis.
	
	☐ Comprehensive reports are prepared and published on a periodic basis (e.g., annual) that are available in different formats (e.g., printed, web-based)
	
	☐ Easy-to-read reports are published on a periodic basis that are customized for use by a diverse audience of interested persons, including reports designed for:
	
	    ○ Agency staff and providers
	    ○ Service recipients, self-advocates and family members
	    ○ General public and funding agents (e.g., legislature)
	
	☐ Published reports include graphics and easy to read tables and are accessible for people with disabilities
	
	☐ Reports clearly identify important trends and patterns, including those that may show poor(er) performance or issues of concern
	
	☐ Narrative in reports contains descriptions and explanations of findings
	
	☐ Reports include benchmarks where available
	
	☐ Reports identify future targets for improvement
	
	☐ Other actions to communicate findings:	

Check (✓) Further Review Needed	STANDARD Description of Data Requirements	NOTES Major Issues and Concerns
☐	**OTHER:**	

IMPROVEMENT PLAN: *Summarize the top 3 issues/problems that are compromising the quality and usefulness of the data you will be or are currently using in your system. Note how these issues can be effectively addressed, who will work on the change and how you will know when the improvement/correction is operational.*

Issue 1:

_____

Improvement Plan:

_____
_____

Who will do it: _____ Timeline: _____

Indicator(s):

_____
_____

Issue 2:

_____

Improvement Plan:

_____

Who will do it: _____ Timeline: _____

Indicator(s):

_____

_____

Issue 3:

_____

Improvement Plan:

_____

_____

Who will do it: _____ Timeline: _____

Indicator(s):

_____

_____

APPENDIX C

Using Data as a Quality Tool in DD

Fixing General Problems with Your Data

Think about your organization's data collection and analysis process to identify the presence of any or all of the following potential problems that can prevent the effective use of data as a quality improvement tool. Summarize the problem making sure to specify which data set(s) is/are the focus of concern.

PROBLEM 1
Absence of a Clear Aim or Goal for Using Data
Evidence this problem is present:

Possible Corrective Action:

PROBLEM 2
Insufficient Statistical Expertise
Evidence this problem is present:

Possible Corrective Action:

PROBLEM 3
Too Much Data
Evidence this problem is present:

Possible Corrective Action:

PROBLEM 4
Internal Organizational Competition
Evidence this problem is present:

Possible Corrective Action:

PROBLEM 5
Complex Data System(s)
Evidence this problem is present:

Possible Corrective Action:

APPENDIX D

CONSIDERATIONS FOR REVIEWING DATA
WITHIN YOUR ORGANIZATION

I. CULTURE. The "culture" within an organization will strongly influence the quality and integrity of the information that is reported by staff regarding a wide range of issues, including those that impact the health and safety of service recipients. This "culture" directly affects staff beliefs concerning the importance of recognizing, reporting and quickly correcting problems. It can vary across the organization and negatively influence the reliability and validity of your data and the accuracy of your analyses. While senior leaders set the tone and expectations that shape this "cultural bias," it is important to recognize that program managers and site supervisors also play an extremely important role. Always ask the following question to help you identify any systems based bias that may be present in your organization's data:

Are there differences in the level of "motivation" to report data?

Question to Consider	If the answer is...	Then a potential problem may exist:
Is the data based on self-report or independent review and reporting?	Self-report	Self-reported data may be less reliable and valid since there is a natural tendency to shy away from reporting information that can reflect poor performance or personal failure. Be cautious when reviewing self-reported data, especially when it focuses on a negative indicator.
Is the reporting voluntary or mandatory?	Voluntary	If voluntary, data reporting may be variable across components of your organization or system. For example, reporting may be considered a high priority by supervisors and managers in one setting, but not be seen as a high priority in other programs. Be careful comparing programs until you know the answer to this question.
Are there consequences for non-reporting?	No	If it "doesn't matter" whether or not reports are made, it may be less likely that data is complete and accurate. Always think about the likelihood of consequences for non-reporting and how that may impact the reliability of the data.
Are they applied consistently?	No	
What are the chances of being "caught?"	Low/none	
If data is reported, is there a potential for negative consequences to the reporter?	Yes	A punitive environment will often suppress reporting since identifying a failure may lead to disciplinary action. Consider whether or not your organization (or even specific managers) has historically used data and information as a punitive and disciplinary tool.
What systems are in place to identify non-reporting or inaccurate reporting?	Few/none	Very often there are not adequate methods in place to measure and assure consistent and accurate reporting. This can lead to reporting errors and an insidious breakdown in the actual implementation of reporting requirements.

128

Question to Consider	If the answer is...	Then this potential problem may exist:
Are there "cultural" differences between organizations/settings with respect to the perceived expectations?	Yes	Different supervisors and managers will stress different aspects of job performance and set informal "expectations" regarding data accuracy and timely reporting. Understand how this can bias the data.

If you identified any of the problems noted above, consider the following SOLUTION:

Change the Organizational Culture: Work to establish an organizational culture that promotes timely reporting of issues for the early identification of problems, so they can be promptly fixed and prevented from happening in the future. This factor is critically important for the establishment of a true culture of safety. It requires changing attitudes and both formal and informal policies that emphasize "catching" staff, "pointing fingers" and "punishing" personnel for errors and systems failures. It can begin by encouraging efforts to highlight positive changes that have resulted from timely reporting and rewarding line personnel, supervisors and program managers who implement solutions that are generated at the local level within your organization, especially those that have been driven by the identification of problems. The development of a more vibrant culture of safety will also be strengthened by the visible "sharing of responsibility" for systems failures by leadership.

OTHER ACTIONS:

II. REPORTER CHARACTERISTICS.
Different people are often responsible for reporting incidents and providing other related data within and across organizations. The role, background and experience, training and responsibility of staff and other reporters can play a critical role in determining the content and accuracy of the data that is reported, analyzed and used to identify issues and make decisions. It is imperative that those who collect, analyze and use data understand the potential for *reporter bias* that may be present. Make sure you ask:

Are there differences in the probability that data will be accurately reported?

Question to Consider	If the answer is…	Then a potential problem may exist:
Who is responsible for collecting data and reporting?	Different People	There may be variations in the level of training, awareness of issues of reliability and data validity. There may also be multiple and conflicting job responsibilities, time constraints and other issues that can interfere with accurate data reporting and that may vary across reporters.
Do people in one group work alone and in the other setting work with multiple staff present?	Yes	This factor is very important for self-reported data such as injury reports, medication errors or other issues that may reflect poorly on the person making the report. When working alone there may be a tendency to under-report when the event suggests an error has been made by the reporter, and especially in instances where an act or failure to act could be construed as neglect or abuse.
Are there any differences in skill or capacity to accurately report?	Yes	Issues such as language skills and cultural backgrounds along with education levels and reading/writing skills can all significantly influence the accuracy of data reports. This is especially true when report forms require staff to interpret terms and concepts that may mean very different things based on one's experience and background.
Is one type of data "easier" to document and report than another?	Yes	Narrative reports can be very difficult for some persons to complete, especially if English is not their primary language or they have limited writing skills. On the other hand, coded forms can be overly complex and difficult to interpret, particularly those with technical terminology. The type of information that is required and the format of how it is reported must be carefully considered when assessing the potential for reporter bias.

IF you identified any of the problems noted above, consider the following SOLUTIONS:

Modify the Reporting Format and Prompts: Consider changing the format and type of information that reporters are required to provide. Try to use less technical and more conventional terminology on report forms (everyday common language). Include 'reporters' in the design of reporting tools and accompanying instructions. Provide instructional sheets that incorporate clear and easy to understand descriptions of terms that can be more readily understood by your staff. Incorporate drop down menus and "pop-up" screens with operational definitions for terms and concepts. Whenever feasible, convert paper forms to an automatic electronic reporting system that directly records and organizes data.

Enhance Training and Support: Provide mandatory initial and periodic refresher instruction for reporters and recorders of data, making sure consistent information is provided across the organization. Use "hands-on" supervised training and/or on-line instruction with practice and feedback methods. Consider orientation and training of service recipients to enhance self-reporting and monitoring of serious incident reporting.

OTHER ACTIONS:

III. DATA ENTRY CONCERNS. Sometimes initial information and data is sent to a second or third party for entry into a database. This often occurs when reports are not electronically generated and therefore the data cannot automatically flow into a data system. Introducing a third party into the flow of information can sometimes help to validate and "error check" information (i.e., reduce variability in recording the data); but, it can also result in additional bias. Therefore, if your reporting system uses separate personnel for data entry (especially if there is more than one data entry staff member), make sure you ask the following question:

What is the probability that data will be accurately documented and entered into a database?

Question to Consider	If the answer is...	Then a potential problem may exist:
Who receives the information for data entry?	Multiple People	The more people involved, the greater the likelihood of error and bias. Each person who "hears" the information or collects the reported data for eventual entry into your database will tend to interpret the data slightly differently. This introduces recorder bias, especially when information is missing or when it is unclear exactly what the reporter wrote or communicated, forcing the recorder to fill in gaps or reassign codes.
Is it the same person who is responsible for entering the data who receives it (e.g., via telephone)?	No	
Is it one individual, or can many different people receive the information and enter the data into a database?	Different People	
Are there differences in how data is communicated and recorded, e.g., sometimes by phone, over the internet, faxing of a form, etc.?	Yes	Narrative reports can be very difficult for some persons to complete, especially if English is not their primary language or they have limited writing skills. On the other hand, coded forms can be overly complex and difficult to interpret, particularly those with technical terminology. The type of information that is required and the format of how it is reported must be carefully considered when assessing the potential for reporter bias.

Question to Consider	If the answer is...	Then a potential problem may exist:
Is the reporting format very complicated or overly technical?	Yes	When reporters experience difficulties completing report forms the information often has to be "corrected" or modified by the data entry person to meet database requirements. This results in an increased potential for error. Assumptions, speculations, and interpretations of "what the reporter really intended" only serve to compromise the reliability of the information.
Is the database or data entry process overly complicated, cumbersome or difficult to interpret?	Yes	Complex data entry processes can lead to incomplete or inaccurate recording. They can also result in frustration on the part of the data entry personnel, prompting shortcuts and inattention. This is not uncommon for older "legacy" data systems. The use of terms and abbreviated headings for data fields that are inconsistent with the language used on report forms will increase the probability of mistakes and errors in entering the data.
Is the language complicated and technical?	Yes	
Is the language for the database different than that used on the report forms?	Yes	
Are there any differences in skill or capacity to accurately record?	Yes	The training and experience of personnel, and their appreciation for how the information is actually used during analysis and to generate reports can significantly contribute to the accuracy and quality of data entry. In addition, awareness of the importance of timely data entry to assure reports are up-to-date is essential. Lags in entry complicate analyses and lead to inaccurate findings and delays in generating reports.

IF you identified any of the problems noted above, consider the following SOLUTIONS:

Define and Clarify Terms and Requirements: Carefully review data reporting terminology and requirements to maximize their alignment (i.e., make sure they mean the same thing and that timelines are the same). Provide operational definitions of terms and use drop-down menus to assure immediate access to definitions, especially when abbreviations are utilized. On a regular basis seek feedback from data entry personnel to identify issues that may be resulting in errors.

Monitor Quality in the System: On a regularly scheduled basis, conduct quality assurance checks of the data to identify gaps, inconsistencies and errors. Review the actual data against expectations (trends and patterns) to identify and study unusual trends and patterns to allow correction of issues that may be resulting in inaccuracies.

Enhance Training and Support: Provide structured training and supervised practice for personnel who are assigned responsibility for data entry. Assure the training includes simulations that provide examples of probable errors and gaps in reporting. Periodically provide refresher training.

Build Teams: Consider creating data analysis teams that include personnel responsible for collecting and entering data along with the analysts who will organize and analyze the data. Have the teams meet on a regular basis to review issues of reliability, validity and usefulness of the data that is being used to generate reports. On a periodic basis include end user representatives (i.e., staff and managers who read and use data reports) and IT personnel who have responsibility for operating, managing and modifying the data systems and databases that are used.

Limit Data Entry Personnel: When direct data entry is not available (i.e., forms are sent to a central location for entry), attempt to limit the number of people who actually enter the data "second-hand" into the system, restrict the number of people who enter the data to increase reliability. When this is not possible, try to provide a "mentoring" system to assure that the same standards are utilized across personnel.

OTHER ACTIONS:

STRATEGIES AND ACTIONS YOU WILL TAKE TO ADDRESS IDENTIFIED ISSUES AND CONCERNS:

APPENDIX E

Using Data as a Quality Improvement Tool

7 COMMON REASONS FOR STAFF ERROR

When thinking about possible causes for failures, consider the following seven (7) common reasons for staff (and others) to experience errors as well as potential factors that may contribute to each type of error. Note that many of the potential contributory factors are really latent faults related to organizational issues. Such latent faults set the stage for later active errors by staff. Once identified, the organization should consider ways to correct them in order to reduce the probability the same types of active errors by staff will occur in the future.

1. **Person doesn't know WHAT to do.** This is a knowledge-based error and can be caused by any number of factors including:
   a. Incomplete instructions, policy or procedure
   b. Confusing or contradictory instructions or procedures
   c. Instructions that are too general and not specific to the person being supported
   d. Reading levels that are too advanced
   e. Inadequate communication
   f. Afraid to ask questions
   g. Routines are confusing or not posted
   h. No training or training was incomplete or not competency based
   i. Information overload – must learn too many different tasks too quickly
   j. Person placed in a new situation and is not familiar with the people, their needs, routines, programs, etc.

2. **Person doesn't know HOW to do it.** This is a skill-based error that can be influenced by all of the factors identified above in no. 1 and also:
   a. Using new or novel equipment
   b. No demonstration of how something is done
   c. Task doesn't occur very often – long period of time since it was last done
   d. Instructions are not readily available or are confusing
   e. No other person available to demonstrate the task
   f. Training material was complex and not based on "hands on" demonstration
   g. Minimal or no opportunity to practice the task under supervision
   h. No supervisory feedback on task performance

3. **Person doesn't know WHY they should do it.** This is an awareness-based error that can have many different causes including:
    a. Lack "big picture" and an understanding of related consequences if something is not done properly
    b. Risk seems too general - not personalized
    c. Risk is viewed as highly unlikely – too rare to be concerned about
    d. Believe their situation is different from others
    e. No prior experience with the risk or consequences
    f. Don't believe it really matters if the task is done differently
    g. Co-workers and supervisors have not stressed the importance of doing the task a certain way

4. **Person FORGETS to do it.** This is a knowledge and/or skill-based error that can be caused by:
    a. Environments that are too "busy" and where activities are "rushed"
    b. Distractions in the environment
    c. Numerous competing demands and activities
    d. Intervening responsibilities or tasks – e.g., suddenly become sidetracked with another service recipient
    e. Limited or No visible cues or prompts that can serve as reminders
    f. Absence of checklists or other "memory aids"
    g. Overly complex instructions or program requirements

5. **Person lacks necessary RESOURCES to do it.** This is often an organization-based error (latent error) that is not uncommon in high-demand DD programs and that can be caused by:
    a. Not enough staff on duty for type of activity
    b. Inadequate, broken or antiquated equipment
    c. Limited supplies and materials
    d. Limited supervision or technical assistance

6. **Person has insufficient TIME to do it.** This too is an organization-based error that can be caused by:
    a. Too many activities or tasks scheduled for a limited time period
    b. Inconsistent work schedule
    c. Routines are not standardized or structured

7. **Person doesn't WANT to do it.** This is a motivation-based error that can be caused by a very wide variety of factors including but not limited to:

   a. Receives little or no recognition for the activity

   b. Task is unpleasant or boring

   c. Task requires more effort and takes more time than other ways of doing something

   d. Task can lead to embarrassment or injury

   e. History of being criticized or "punished" if they make a mistake

   f. Interferes with more desirable activities

   g. Want to avoid interactions with others involved in task

The identified "reason(s)" will determine what "solutions" should be considered to reduce the probability the same type of error will take place in the future.

APPENDIX F

CHECKLIST FOR REVERSE ENGINEERING DATA MANAGEMENT SYSTEMS

A Guide to the Design of Data Reporting and Analysis

The checklist below is designed to be a first step in "reverse engineering" the development of your data reports and associated data analysis. The checklist is intended to be completed by end users (e.g., leadership, managers) of proposed data analyses and reports. To complete the checklist respondents should answer the following key questions that can help direct data development activities. They should try to be as specific as possible. Focus and clarity of need are critical. Reports and analyses will be most relevant and useful when guided by a clear understanding of your information related needs.

Purpose: Why do you want a report?

WHAT is the strategic goal associated with the proposed data report? If more than one goal is identified, list the top 3 below:

1.
2.
3.

WHY do you want the data?

☐ **Describe** (e.g., population characteristics/demographics)

☐ **Evaluate** (e.g., performance, service quality, client satisfaction)

☐ **Compare** (e.g., against benchmarks or targets, between client groups or by risk factors, differences by service, regions or provider)

☐ **Track trends over time** (e.g., access, requests for services, needs, mortality rates)

☐ **Identify risks** (e.g., identify patterns, risk factors, targets for intervention)

☐ **Assess costs** (e.g., costs for services, labor, providers)

☐ **Project future** (e.g., future trends, changes in population characteristics, downsizing initiatives)

☐ **Set Goals** (e.g., improvement targets, goals for reduction in incidents/adverse events)

☐ **Choose services or providers** (e.g., use information in provider selection process)

☐ **Other** (specify):

WHAT are the KEY QUESTIONS you want the data to answer? What do you want to be analyzed? Be as specific as possible. [Note: this will most likely evolve over time as you review the actual data and results of analysis.]

137

Audience: Who is the report for?

WHO do you want to <u>use</u> the data?

- ☐ Senior leadership
- ☐ Division or unit managers
- ☐ Health care and/or clinical personnel
- ☐ Field managers/supervisors
- ☐ Line staff
- ☐ Quality and/or risk management personnel
- ☐ Service Providers
- ☐ Support recipients (persons with ID/DD)
- ☐ Family members of service recipients and/or advocates
- ☐ Other (specify):

WHO else do you want to share the data with?

- ☐ State or federal funding agencies
- ☐ Governmental agencies (e.g., CDC, AHRQ)
- ☐ Board(s) of Directors
- ☐ Public or private service providers
- ☐ Trade organizations
- ☐ Service recipients/consumers/families
- ☐ Health care professionals or organizations (e.g., hospitals or clinics)
- ☐ Public (e.g., newspapers)
- ☐ Other (specify):

OPTIONAL: Your goals may vary for each of the audience groups you have identified above. This may result in the need to plan for different strategies in communicating data depending upon who is the intended recipient. To help "think about" how your reporting of data might vary, begin to make notes about why you might want to provide different information to your important audiences, i.e., how do you think they might benefit from reviewing the data and how much and what kind of data would be most useful to them? Select only the top three groups to begin with. Over time you can expand your planning.

How You Will Focus Data by Audience Category

Audience	Why they should review it What is the purpose of their review – what do you hope to achieve from their review?	Type of data (level of detail - important limitations/considerations in presenting data)

138

Method: How you will communicate/publish the data?

The exact method for reporting data will obviously vary depending how you want it to be used (purpose) and what your intended audience is. Many I/DD organizations use multiple report formats including annual reports (that provide comprehensive information) and shorter but more frequent "briefs" or newsletters that contain a limited but focused amount of information. For the top five (3) audiences listed in the table above, select the report style and frequency that you believe may be most appropriate. You can always change your selections after you have had a chance to actually review the format and feedback from users.

Audience	How the data should be provided (What format makes the most sense for the selected audience?)	When –frequency– (How often should the data be provided?)

WHEN (how often) do you want to receive the data?

☐ Real time (whenever needed)
☐ Daily
☐ Weekly
☐ Monthly
☐ Semi-annually
☐ Once a year
☐ Other: _____

WHAT is the specific population or service area you want the data to address?
(List specific characteristics such as diagnosis, eligibility status, age range, type of services received, geographic area, etc.)

WHAT time period do you want the data to reflect? (Be highly specific – is it a point in time, for the past six months, one year – fiscal year or calendar year, etc.)

139

HOW do you want the data presented?

☐ Itemized List (list of raw data in columns and rows)

☐ Tables (listing of specific data by pre-defined categories)

☐ Graphs (line, pie or bar graphs to visually illustrate the data)

☐ Narrative (written description of the data)

☐ Other (specify): _____

ILLUSTRATE your ideas on presenting the data (e.g., if you have an idea, sketch below what a table/chart should look like):

WHAT level of DETAIL do you want in the data report? Specify the approximate level of detail you are looking for, e.g., only summary data, case specific data, averages, range (highest to lowest), everything.

Do you want the data ANALYZED? Specify the type of analysis you want, if any. If you are unsure about what type of analyses would be most useful, write down below the most important questions you want to be able to answer with the data report.

ADDITIONAL INFORMATION:

Approximately how many pages do you want?

Do you want a draft or prototype report to review first? ☐ Yes   ☐ No

Who should be contacted for clarification if questions arise re: the content or format for the report?

Are there any examples of reports that you would like this report to look like? If yes, provide references and/or attach samples:

ADDITIONAL COMMENTS OR INSTRUCTIONS:

Appendix G

SUMMARY DATA ANALYSIS PLAN

Complete the following information in as much detail as possible before beginning a new or enhanced analysis of data. Share it with end users and leadership within your organization to help clarify needs and expectations. If available, refer back to the **Checklist for Reverse Engineering Data Management Systems** to assure alignment and access background information.

WHAT are the KEY QUESTIONS that are being asked and that the data can answer? Be as specific as possible and note what questions can and cannot be addressed with available data. Highlight questions that end users and leadership have indicated are priorities.

_____
_____
_____
_____
_____
_____
_____
_____
_____
_____

WHAT is the estimated VALIDITY and RELIABILITY of the data that you anticipate using for the analysis? Identify issues and limitations of the data.

_____
_____
_____
_____
_____
_____
_____
_____

ARE there OTHER sources of data and information that can be used to help answer the question(s)? Note them below along with a summary of any concerns or special issues (e.g., consistency, effort, access).

_____

_____

_____

_____

_____

_____

WHAT is the estimated resource commitment that will be needed to complete this analysis? (List anticipated staff, funding, additional resource needs and realistic time lines for completing the analysis.)

_____

_____

_____

_____

_____

ADDITIONAL COMMENTS OR INSTRUCTIONS:

Reviewed by: (List below who should review this plan):

Appendix H

Examples for Using a Chi-square Test

EXAMPLE 1: The following example illustrates how to conduct a Chi-square test of independence with two groups of data, each of which has two levels. In this example, a service provider organization wants to answer the following question: *"Is the pattern of restraint use the same in Area 2 as Area 1?"* In other words, is the pattern of restraint independent of program area? The data for inclusion in the analysis is as follows:

Number of People			
Location	Restrained	Not Restrained	Total
Area 1	25	601	626
Area 2	34	800	834
Total	59	1401	1460

The first step in the analysis requires the calculation of expected frequencies using the row and column totals in the table as follows:

- To calculate the expected frequency of persons who were restrained for Area 1 multiply the total number of people from the first area (626) by the total number of people restrained for both areas (59) divided by the total number of people (restrained and not restrained) across both areas (1460).

- To calculate the expected frequency of persons who were not restrained for Area 1, multiply the total number of people in Area 1 (626) times the total number of people not restrained in both areas (1401) divided by the total number of people who were restrained and not restrained across both areas. Repeat these calculations for Area 2. The table below illustrates these calculations for the expected frequencies:

Expected Frequencies

	Number of People	
Location	Restrained	Not Restrained
Area 1	626*59/1460= 25.3	626*1401/1460= 600.7
Area 2	834*59/1460= 33.7	834*1401/1460= 800.3

Then, for each cell, calculate: (observed – expected)^2 / expected and add these calculations together, as follows:

$$(25-25.3)\,^2/25.3 + (34-33.7)\,^2/33.7 + (601-600.7)\,^2/601 + (800-800.3)\,^2/800.3 = \mathbf{0.00637}$$

Another way to calculate this is to use a simple 2X2 table such as illustrated below. This method eliminates the extra step of calculating expected frequencies.

	Number of People		
Location	Restrained	Not Restrained	Total
Area 1	a	b	
Area 2	c	d	
Total			Total

Special Note: this method only works when comparing two factors, each with two levels.

$$\chi^2 \text{ (chi-square)} = Total * (a*d – b*c)^2 / (a*b*c*d)$$

$$\chi^2 = 1460* (25*800-601*34)^2 /(25*601*34*800) = \mathbf{0.00637}$$

After completing these calculations, compare the obtained value to the χ^2 (chi-square) distribution with degrees of freedom = 1 (# of rows -1)*(# of columns - 1). For a 2X2 table, the degrees of freedom[v] are always equal to 1. The χ^2 critical value is **3.841** (this value is obtained from a chart).[vi] If

---

[v] Degrees of Freedom is a statistical unit that indicates the lack of restriction in calculations, or the number of values in a calculation that are free to vary. It is used to help establish the significance of statistical results.

[vi] A table of values can be accessed from the Pennsylvania State University which publishes a free Chi-Square Distribution table online (see: http://sites.stat.psu.edu/~mga/401/tables/Chi-square-table.pdf.) Other internet online tables can be found by using search terms "Chisquare distribution table"

the calculated χ2 is greater than the critical value, it suggests that there is enough evidence to conclude that there is likely a difference in the number of restraints between areas 1 and 2. In our example, however, the calculated χ2 = 0.00637. This value is much less than the critical value. Therefore, it can be concluded that there is likely <u>not</u> a significant difference in the number of restraints between areas 1 and 2; i.e., the rate of restraint is independent of area.

EXAMPLE 2: The second example illustrates how to use the chi-square test of independence to test the difference between two years of data. Assume a private provider wants to answer the following question: *"Is the number of people restrained the same this year as it was last year?"* In other words, is the pattern of restraint independent of the year?

Number of People			
Time Period	Restrained	Not Restrained	Total
Previous Year	52	800	852
Current Year	59	1401	1460
Total	111	2201	2312

Use the simplified version of the formula from Example 1 above:

$$\chi^2 = 2312 * (52*1401-800*59)2 / (52*800*59*1401) = \mathbf{5.006}$$

The calculated χ2 is larger than the critical value of 3.841. Thus one can conclude that there <u>is</u> a significant difference between years. When examining the restraints together with the size of the population, we see that while there were more restraints in the current year (59) than the previous year (52), the population also increased substantially between the two years. As a result, the rate of restraints is significantly lower in the second year than in the previous year. The rate is a better measure in this instance since the population changed so dramatically between the two years.

> **CAUTION:** If any of the cell sizes of the expected values are less than 5, the Chi-square test should <u>not</u> be used as the results may not be valid

Appendix I

Example for Calculating Student's t-test

While there are different types of t-tests, this example will focus on the *Student's t-test* for a sample of unpaired data - a relatively common type of data analysis present in I/DD organizations and service systems. Remember: always consult with a statistician when unsure of what test should be used for specific sets of data that will be analyzed.

Calculation of the t-statistic requires the following information associated with these sample questions:

1. *What is the presumed value of the difference between the means?* For example, if testing to see whether or not there's evidence that the means of two data sets are equal (e.g., ages of service recipients for two different years), then the *presumed* difference would be zero.

2. *Is the variance of the populations the same?* Often, we don't know enough about whether the value we're measuring has the same variance in the population from year-to-year, or between two different groups. In this case, we can use a formula designed for unequal variances. When in doubt, use the *t-test for unequal variances*. With this adjusted formula, one is less likely to conclude the populations have a statistically significant difference – this will reduce the probability of making a faulty conclusion.

3. *Is the population normally distributed?* Often we don't have enough information to know the distribution of the data in the population. While this particular statistical test was designed for a normally distributed population, it's still useful for populations with other distributions as long as we have enough information. We'll want to make sure each set of data has at least 30 entries to use this test if we're not sure the information is normally distributed.

To calculate the statistic, it is first necessary to calculate the mean and the standard deviation of each group of data. Then enter this information into the following formula:

$$t = \frac{\text{mean group 1} - \text{mean group 2} - \text{tested difference}}{\sqrt{\dfrac{\text{standard deviation group 1}^2}{\text{number of data points group 1}} + \dfrac{\text{standard deviation group 2}^2}{\text{number of data points group 2}}}}$$

Note: a video demonstration that illustrates how to perform this calculation is included in the on-line course entitled *Using Data as a Quality Tool in DD* which is part of the *Risk Management in DD* series of on-line courses available at: http://www.udiscovering.org.

Interpreting Results. To determine statistical significance, the calculated t statistic is compared to a "critical" value of t taken from the t-distribution (values are available on-line or in published charts in most statistics books). It should be noted that there are different versions of t distribution tables that can provide the corresponding value of t. This example uses one published by UCLA and that is available free of charge at the following link: **http://www.socr.ucla.edu/applets.dir/t-table.html**[vii]

When the populations being compared have <u>equal</u> variances, the calculated value of t is compared to the *critical* value from the t distribution that corresponds to the sum of the number of observations from each group minus two (called the degrees of freedom) in our t distribution table. For example, if we have 30 observations in each group, the degrees of freedom are: $30 + 30 - 2 = 58$.

Testing the difference at a 0.05 level of significance (i.e., a 95% probability the observed difference is not due to chance and would be found again), requires a t critical value of 1.67 for a one-direction comparison, or 2.00 for a two-direction comparison (taken from the t distribution table). In a two-direction comparison, we are testing whether the group 2 mean is either above or below the group 1 mean. In a one-direction comparison, we're only testing whether the groups are different in one direction – for example, whether the mean of group 2 is greater than group 1.

When conducting a t-test for <u>unequal</u> population variances, an *adjusted t* is calculated. Since this can be a little more complex, it is often easier to use statistical calculators usually available within a spreadsheet program (as is shown in the demonstration video in the on-line course). The adjusted t critical value uses two values of t, each corresponding to the number of observations from each group minus 1. To do this first calculate the following ratio for each group (we'll call it "w1" for group 1):

$$w1 = \frac{(\text{standard deviation group 1})^2}{\text{number of data points in group 1}}$$

Next, use the ratio (w) in the following formula:

$$\text{adjusted } t = \frac{(w1 \times t_{\text{group 1}}) + (w2 \times t_{\text{group 2}})}{w1 + w2}$$

The value of t that is calculated for this data is then compared to the appropriate *critical* values of t. If the calculated t is equal to or greater than the critical value there is enough evidence to suggest that the two groups of data have a statistically significant difference in their mean values. If the

---

[vii] Statistics Online Computational Resource (SOCR) provides access to a wide variety of statistical resources and tables that are available for use by the public by going to: http://www.SOCR.ucla.edu.

calculated t is less than the critical value of t there is not have enough evidence to suggest that the means are different.

CAUTION: This test should <u>not</u> be used on very small sample sizes (less than 30 entries in each group) when the distribution of the value in the population is either unknown or is known to not be normally distributed. Using the test incorrectly can lead to inaccurate analytic findings. Consult with a qualified statistician whenever there is uncertainty about what test to use.

APPENDIX J

How to Calculate an Age-adjusted Rate

There are two basic ways to adjust for the age distribution within a population: (a) direct age adjustment and (b) indirect adjustment. The latter is used when data on the outcome of interest is not available for each specific age group.

DIRECT AGE ADJUSTMENT

Age adjustment provides a statistical method for adjusting the data of at least one of the populations being compared in order to understand what the statistics about a particular outcome, such as mortality, might look like if both populations had the same age distribution. Thus, age adjustment is used to help answer the question: *"Is the difference in outcome rate between two populations due only to age, or is it due to factors other than age?"* When comparing certain outcomes (such as mortality or morbidity) for the service recipient population of an I/DD organization to the general population it can be especially important to answer this question since there are often substantial differences in age between the two groups.

In national and state mortality statistics the age distribution of the 2000 U.S. Standard Population is often used as a way to weight the mortality statistics for each age group. However, when comparing only two distinct populations, it is sometimes preferable to adjust the statistics to the age distribution of one of those populations, as opposed to the U.S. general population. For example, if comparing data from one service provider to another, the first provider's data can be adjusted for the age distribution of the second provider. This can help reduce the probability that age differences were responsible for obtained differences in the outcome measure being reviewed.

When considering age adjustment, it is important to recognize that the age distribution of a population can change over time. Therefore, when comparing an outcome like mortality over time, it may be preferable to age-adjust the statistics at each time period to ensure that perceived changes in mortality rates are not due to a change in the underlying age distribution (e.g., aging of the population, or even an influx of younger people).

As noted, in the direct method of age adjustment, the age distribution of one population is used to eliminate the effects of any actual differences in age distributions on the outcome statistics under review. As an example of how this is done consider mortality within an I/DD population. To standardize, the mortality rates are calculated for each age group (e.g., 10 year age groups) for the population that will be standardized. These mortality rates are applied to the standard population to determine the number of people that would be *expected* to die at these rates (if the age distribution were the same). Then, the total number of expected deaths is summed up over the age groups, divided by the total standard population size and multiplied by the rate unit (e.g., multiplied by 1000 if the rate unit is 'per 1000 people'). The resulting mortality rate represents the expected mortality rate for the population if it had the age distribution of the standard population.

150

CALCULATING A DIRECT AGE ADJUSTMENT.   First, one must decide which rate is to be adjusted. As described earlier, when comparing rates of an outcome from two populations, you can either adjust both to the age distribution of a common population (such as the U.S. Standard Population), or adjust the rate of one to the other. When comparing two I/DD systems, this second option may be most useful as it requires only that the rate for one system is adjusted as if it had the age distribution of the second.

Next, the data is broken up into age groups. The same age groups must be used within each dataset. The age groups do not have to be equally spaced, although it is common practice to use 5 or 10 year increments.

In the example presented below, the mortality rate of Group B will be adjusted to the age distribution of Group A. Note that without adjustment, the mortality rate of Group B (14.9 per thousand) is lower than that of Group A (16.0 per thousand). The table below presents the age distribution for the first group (A).

Population for Group A		
Age Group	No. People	Percent of People in Age Group
0 to 4	1160	11.6%
5 to 14	1400	14.0%
15 to 24	960	9.6%
25 to 34	1360	13.6%
35 to 44	1630	16.3%
45 to 54	1350	13.5%
55 to 64	870	8.7%
65 to 74	660	6.6%
75 to 84	450	4.5%
85+	160	1.6%W
Total	10,000	100%

The percentage of the population each age group is then used as a *weight* to adjust the rate of mortality for the second group (B). In the table illustrated on the next page the number of deaths and the population in each age group for Group B are used to calculate an unadjusted age-specific mortality rate. This rate is then multiplied by the *weight* to create an adjusted rate for each age group.

| Age Group | Group B | | | Group A | Group B |
	No. Deaths (a)	Population (b)	Unadjusted Age-specific Rate per 1,000 c = (a ÷ b) x 1,000	Weight (d)	Weighted Rate (c x d)
0 to 4	12	1000	12.0	0.116	1.39
5 to 14	14	2000	7.0	0.140	0.98
15 to 24	22	5000	4.4	0.096	0.42
25 to 34	21	5500	3.8	0.136	0.52
35 to 44	32	4500	7.1	0.163	1.116
45 to 54	75	5500	13.6	0.135	1.84
55 to 64	90	3300	27.3	0.087	2.37
65 to 74	45	1500	30.0	0.066	1.98
75 to 84	60	640	93.8	0.045	4.22
85+	16	120	133.3	0.016	2.13
Total	387	26,060	**14.9**	1,000	**17.0**

To calculate the age-adjusted rate, add the weighted rates for each age group. As shown in the table above, Group B's adjusted mortality rate would be 17.0 per thousand. This means that if Group B had the same age distribution as Group A, we estimate that the mortality rate would be 17.0 per thousand. Then compare the mortality rate for Group A to the mortality rate for Group B. The age-adjusted rate for Group B is higher than the unadjusted rate of 14.9 per thousand because Group A had a higher proportion of people in the oldest age groups, where the mortality rates were the highest. By weighting these rates more heavily during the adjustment to align with Group A's population distribution by age, the adjusted mortality rate increased. This means that if Group B had more of the population in older age groups the way Group A does, the mortality rate would likely be higher.

Risk adjustment can be performed for factors other than age using a similar methodology. The population should be split into subgroups. The rate of a particular outcome can then be waited in a similar fashion.

LIMITATIONS. It's important to recognize that such age adjustment is only an estimate, and that while the mortality rate is adjusted for age, other factors may differ in the populations that substantially affect the risk of death. While adjustment can be performed for other factors known to affect mortality (such as sex, race, ambulation, chronic illness, etc.), it is usually best not to select a comparison population that's drastically different from your population of study with regard to mortality risk. Remember that the estimates are only hypothetical since they are based on a sample population and therefore really do not have the ability to reflect the true mortality risk of that population.

INDIRECT AGE ADJUSTMENT

A second form of age adjustment is referred to as *indirect adjustment*. Sometimes it is also called a *standardized mortality ratio*. This method of adjustment is useful when the number of deaths per age group is not available. In this method, the age-specific mortality rates from a comparison population are applied to the age-specific population being examined to estimate the *expected* number of deaths in the population, i.e., how many deaths would be expected to have taken place if it had the same mortality profile as the comparison population. The total expected deaths are then compared to the observed number of deaths in a ratio called a *standardized mortality ratio* (SMR):

SMR = Observed Number of Deaths Expected/Number of Deaths

This ratio is often multiplied by 100 to eliminate decimals and make the number easier to understand. A ratio of 1 (or 100 if multiplied) suggests that the observed number of deaths is similar to the expected number of deaths. A ratio of less than 1 (or less than 100) suggests that the observed number of deaths is less than the expected number of deaths. Conversely, a ratio of greater than 1 (or over 100) suggests the observed number of deaths is greater than the expected number of deaths.

This method can be useful when examining mortality (or another outcome) over time in the same population of people with I/DD. The mortality rate from the previous year can be used to calculate the *expected* number of deaths for the current year:

Previous mortality rate (per 1000) * Current Year Population / 1000 = Expected number of deaths for current year

APPENDIX K

Sample Tables for Presenting
Descriptive Statistical Analyses of Typical I/DD Data

The following tables and sample graphs are provided to illustrate some relatively basic means of organizing and presenting descriptive analysis of data for service systems and organizations that support people with I/DD. The examples that are provided are not intended to be exhaustive of all possibilities, but rather reflect a few ways of presenting data that the authors have found to be useful and easy to understand by a wide range of readers.

Age Distribution

Since age is an important risk factor for many health-related outcomes and since the distribution of service recipients by age is not uniform, it is important to include age in the analysis of certain types of data. The use of standard conventions for grouping age is also recommended, as this will allow you to compare your findings with those typically present in national and state databases.

EXAMPLE: Distribution of a Health-related Outcome by Age Group

Age Range	No. with outcome	Percent with outcome	Crude Rate (No. per 1000)
18-24 yrs			
25-34 yrs			
35-44 yrs			
45-54 yrs			
55-64 yrs			
65-74 yrs			
75-84 yrs			
85 yrs & older			
Total		**100%**	

1. First calculate the actual number of people with the outcome in the time period under study (e.g., one year) for each of the listed age groups.
2. Next calculate the percentage of the total people with the outcome represented by each of the age groups (no. of people with outcome in the age group/total no. of people with the outcome X 100%).
3. Next, calculate the number of people in your population during the time period under study (the same time period used in step 1) for the listed age groups. This data will be used in step 4.
4. Finally calculate the crude rate using a standard unit of measurement (e.g. the people with the outcome per 1000 people). This is done by dividing the number of people with the outcome for each age group by the number of persons in the population in that group and then multiplying by 1,000. [If there were 15 people with the flu in the first age group and 700 people in that age

154

group, the rate of flu per 1000 people would be equal to (15/700)*1000, or 2.1 cases of flu per 1000 people.]

5. One or more graphs of the data can be created. Percent of cases of flu by age group may be best indicated by a pie chart or dot chart. Rates can be presented using a column or bar graph (horizontal axis = age categories).

> **Note:** Use of a spreadsheet program, such as Microsoft Excel, can facilitate the analysis of your data and greatly enhance the presentation of standard tables and graphs.

Data by Type of Service or Residential Setting

Tables for service type and type of residential setting are commonly used in I/DD service systems and organizations. These tables need to reflect the specific categories that any given system or agency already uses. The samples presented below are generic in nature and will need to be adapted to the categories and labels used in your organization. Therefore, they are only examples of how you can illustrate your data.

EXAMPLE: Satisfaction with services by Type of Residential Setting or Service Type

Residential Setting or Service Type	Population (No. People)	% of Population	Avg. hours of staffing per week	No. Satisfied	Percent Satisfied	Rate of Satisfaction (n/1000)
Type 1						
Type 2						
Type 3						
Type 4						
Type 5						
Total		100%			100%	
Average						

1. It is important to first determine the categories that you want to compare and that will be illustrated in the data table above. Make sure you have your population and measured data organized in a fashion that is consistent with these categories. Enter the labels in column 1.
   a. For residential settings, categories might include: institutional program, community group living, private or community group living, public, foster care, out of home independent living, at home with family, etc.
   b. For service type, categories might include: case management only, family support, self-directed funding, community residence, vocational services/no residence, etc. Make sure the categories reflect what is commonly used in your organization.

2. Second, calculate the population for each of the categories that are listed in the first column for the time period under review and put that in the second column.
3. It is helpful to calculate the percentage of the total population in each of the service types or residential settings listed in the first column. This can provide context and help readers better appreciate the relative distribution of your population included in each of those categories. Percentages are determined by dividing the number of people in each service or residential type by the total service population and then multiplying by 100%.
4. OPTIONAL: Display characteristics of each setting or service that may be relevant to the interpretation of the data. In our example of satisfaction levels across services, it may be important to understand, for example, the relative amount of support received in each setting – shown here as the average hours of services per week. Information like this can provide a useful reference regarding relative findings.
5. Then calculate the actual number of measured items (e.g. events, outcomes, satisfaction) that took place in the time period under review for people receiving services in each setting or type. Be careful of duplicated counts.
6. Next, calculate the percentage of the data represented by each of the categories to illustrate the relative proportion for each setting or service type. This is calculated by entering the number of measured items/total number of measured items X 100 for each category.
7. Finally, calculate a rate using a standard unit of measurement (in this case the satisfaction per 1,000 people). This is done by dividing the number of measured items for each group by the number of persons in the population in that group and then multiplying by 1,000.
8. Multiple graphs of the data can be created. In order to facilitate reading of the graphs, it is recommended that graphs use common units of measurement for the vertical axis.

Trends over Time

One of the first questions that is usually asked by leadership and other stakeholders has to do with temporal trends, in other words, what change if any is taking place over time, or "Is it getting better or worse?" The table below represents a relatively simple way to organize and display your data to illustrate trends. The use of a crude rate is essential to this type of presentation when the service population or group being measured varies in size over time.

Example: Trends for the Calendar Years 2008 - 2012

Year	Population	No. Outcomes	Outcome Rate (No. outcomes/1000)
2008			
2009			
2010			
2011			
2012			

1. Identify the time periods that you will be using and enter them into the first column. [Calendar years usually start on January 1st and end on December 31st. Fiscal years are determined by your organization. Common Fiscal Years run either between July 1st and June 30th or October 1st to September 30th.] Make sure you use the same time convention for all of your analyses. In addition, it is extremely helpful to use the time period for analysis that is used for other organizational reports (e.g., incident reports, quality reports, demographic reports, fiscal reports) in order to allow eventual cross factor comparisons and analyses. It is more likely that population data will also be more readily available for these time periods as well.

2. Second, calculate the population for and the number of measured items that took place in each of the time periods that are listed in the first column, put those figures in the second and third columns, respectively.

3. Then calculate the rate for each time period using the formulas discussed above (number of measured items/population X 1000).

4. OPTIONAL: Use additional columns to show other important factors across the years in order to provide context and perspective.

Categorical Rankings with Comparisons (Benchmarks)

Examining relative changes over time with regard to the ranking of categorical data can be very useful to understand your data, both within your sphere of responsibility and as compared to selected benchmarks. This can help identify shifts in categories that may warrant more intensive examination. When using benchmarking data, carefully select data that will not result in a biased comparison.

Example: Comparison of the Top 5 Reasons for Emergency Room Visits
For 3 Years and with Other DD Service Systems

Rank	Comparative Data 1 for Current Year	Comparative Data 2 for Current Year	Your organization		
			Past Year 2	Past Year 1	Current Year (20XX)
1	Cause XX%	Cause XX%	Cause XX%	Cause XX%	Cause XX%
2					
3					
4					
5					

1. Identify the time periods and comparative data that you will be using. The table assumes data for 3 years within your organization. Comparative data is displayed only for the current year. [It is certainly possible to reconfigure the table to include a year by year analysis of data from your organization with comparison groups.] Pay special attention to differences that may exist between your data and that provided in comparative datasets. To the extent possible, use comparable time

periods. Where substantial differences exist that may influence the comparison, make sure these are clearly noted in the report text and provided in footnotes.

2. The table above assumes that the data for each cause will be presented as a percentage of the total number of ER visits. The cause with the highest percentage is given the number 1 rank, and so on. Each box within the table includes both the name of cause and its percentage.

An additional method for illustrating changes in the cause-specific rates of ER visits within your organization over time is illustrated in the table below.

Example: Trends for Leading Causes of ER Visits
20XX – 20XX

Current Rank	Previous Ranking	Cause of ER Visit	Rates of Visits (per 1,000) for Your Organization		
			20XX Past Year 2	20XX Past Year 1	20XX Current Year
1	1				
2	2				
3	4				
4	3				
5	6				

Any number of alternatives is possible for illustrating this type of data. What is important is that the tables and any accompanying graphs help your readers to understand the relative rankings in terms of causes of ER visits within your population, major changes that seem to be taking place over time (or across other service recipient or organizational factors) and differences that may exist between your population and comparative groups in terms of what are the leading causes of ER visits. Understanding these variations can help you to better target areas for more detailed examination and quality improvement.

Made in the USA
Las Vegas, NV
23 June 2021